Ecology for All Ages

ECOLOGY
FOR ALL AGES

*Discovering Nature through Activities
for Children and Adults*

by

Jorie Hunken

The
Globe
Pequot
Press

Old Saybrook, Connecticut

Library of Congress Cataloging-in-Publication Data

Hunken, Jorie.
      Ecology for all ages: discovering nature through activities for children and adults / by Jorie
Hunken — 1st ed.
          p.   cm.
      Includes index.
      ISBN 1-56440-138-3
      1. Ecology—Study and teaching—Activity programs. 2. Habitat (Ecology)—Study and teaching.
I. Title.
QH541.2.H86 1994
574.5'26—dc20   93-11969
                                                                                              CIP

Text design by Nancy Freeborn

Art credits: Page 62: Heather Brack; page 149: David Longland.
All others by the author.

Manufactured in the United States of America
First Edition/First Printing

Contents

Introduction, ix

Backyard Ecology

Areas of Heavy Use: School Yards, Suburban Yards, Playgrounds, and Parks, 1

Characteristics of the Area, 2
Common Inhabitants, 2

Looking Carefully at What Lives Nearby, 8
  1. Keeping an Explorer's Journal, 8
  2. Plant Places, 9
  3. Signs of Animals in Your Area, 10
  4. Small Seek, 13
  5. Choosing a Personal Habitat, 15

Wear and Repair—The Interaction of People, Plants, Creatures, and the Elements, 16
  6. Hard Land, Soft Land, 16
  7. Soil on the Run, 18
  8. Be an Erosion Detective, 19
  9. Excavators in the Ecosystem, 20
  10. Cashing in on the Riches of Disturbed Soil, 21

Changes in the Neighborhood Ecosystem, 23
  11. Succession in the Backyard, 24
  12. Berry Bush "Strategies," 26
  13. The House That Nature Built, 27

Litter, 28
  14. Analyzing Natural Leaf Litter, 28
  15. Evidence of the Human Litterbug, 29
  16. The Unrottables and the Rottables, 30
  17. The Compost Pile—Nature's Recycling System, 31
  18. Eco-nomics: Buying into Recycling, 32

Water Systems

Still or Moving Water: Ponds, Lakes, Brooks, Rivers, and Creeks, 35

Streams—Water on the Move, 37

Characteristics of the Area, 37
Common Inhabitants, 37

Observing Water Flow, 40
  1. Making a Model Streambed, 41
  2. Discovering How Water Carves Out Habitats, 43

Survival in Streams, 45
  3. Exploring Brook Habitats, 45
  4. Streamlining: An Adaptation for Survival, 46
  5. Discovering How Streamlining Works, 47

The Balance of Life in a Stream, 47
  6. How Topsoil Loss Affects Our Fields and Forests, 47
  7. An Overdose of Nutrients: Algae Overgrowth, 48

Ponds—Quiet Water, 51

Characteristics of the Area, 51
Common Inhabitants, 52

Studying the Area, 52
  8. Taking a Pond Life Survey, 54

The Water's Surface, 56
  9. Experimenting with Surface Tension, 57
  10. Clustered Interaction on the Water, 58

Breathing Under Water, 59
  11. Solutions for Getting a Breath Under Water, 59

Feeding in and around Ponds, 61
  12. Adaptations of Predators, 61
  13. Dragonflies: The Falcons of the Pond, 62
  14. Looking for Signs of Feeding at the Edge of the Pond, 64
  15. Baiting and Marking to Observe Behaviors, 66

Escaping Predation, 67
   16. Making Models of Camouflaged Pond Animals, 67
   17. Pond Swim Meet: Shapes and Devices of
      Swimmers, 68

The Foundation of the Pond Food Chain, 70
   18. Pond Plants—Charting their Habitats and Adaptations, 70
   19. Aquatic Micro-Monsters, 72
   20. Food Chains: The House That Jack Built, 73

The Seasonal Reunion, 74
   21. Looking for Signs of Breeding, 74

The Watershed, 75
   22. Using Maps to Study Your Watershed, 75
   23. Charting the Effects of Acid Rain, 76

Fields and Borders

Pastures, Prairies, Edges of Playing Fields, and Vacant Lots, 79

Characteristics of the Area, 80
Common Inhabitants, 80

Plants Create a Field of Energy, 85
   1. Turning Sunlight into Sugar and Passing It On, 85
   2. How Plants Make Food, 86
   3. Adaptations of Leaves That Live in the Open, 88

Pollination, 89
   4. What Insects Get from Plants, 89
   5. What Plants Get from Insects, 90
   6. Flowers as Signs and Signals—A Pollinator's Treasure Hunt, 92
   7. Being a Bee, 94

Plants on the Move, Plants Settled Down, 95
   8. Flying Seeds, 95
   9. Hitchhiking Seeds, 96
   10. Identifying Plant Colonies, 96

The Field Habitat in Transition, 98
   11. Field Surveys: Looking for Evidence of Future
      Changes, 98

Needs and Niches, 100
   12. Measuring Plant Diversity, 100
   13. Looking for Clues of Alliances and Interactions, 102
   14. Meadow Mouse Signs, 103
   15. Requirements for Healthy Habitats, 104
   16. How Do Butterflies Help Ecologists?, 105
   17. Establishing a Claim: The Field's Resources, 106
   18. Strands of Interrelationships: Making an Energy-
      Transfer Diagram, 108

Human Use of Energy Resources, 109
   19. How Do We Get What We Need?, 109
   20. Reading an Electric Meter, 111
   21. How We Can Cut Back on Our Energy Use, 113
   22. Energy-Efficient Eating Habits, 115

Trees and the Woods

Woodlots and Forests, 117

Characteristics of the Area, 118
Common Inhabitants, 119

The Life Processes of a Tree, 123
   1. How a Branch Grows, 123
   2. Finding the Living Tissues of a Tree, 124
   3. How Roots Grow, 125
   4. How Water Moves Through a Tree, 126

A Tree's Life History, 127
   5. What Happens When a Tree Dies?, 127
   6. Comparing Trees, 129

Trees and the Seasons, 130
   7. Forcing Spring Buds in Winter, 130
   8. Flowering Pines and Flying Pine Seeds, 131
   9. Finding Tree Seeds, 133
   10. Nut Collecting, 134
   11. Sprouting Found Nuts, 135
   12. Understanding Color Changes in Leaves, 135

Trees as Homes for Other Organisms, 136
   13. Looking for Plants that Live on Trees, 136
   14. Finding Insects That Live Inside Leaves, 138
   15. Caterpillars and Trees, 139

16. Captive Caterpillars, 141
17. Birds of the Woods Report, 143
18. Old Trees as Homesites, 144
19. Time Traveling: Looking for Clues of Past and
    Future Events, 145
20. Finding a Home in the Woods, 146

Woodland Mushrooms: Essential Participants, 146
21. Mycorrhizae: The Partnership of Fungi and Trees, 147

Life in the Woodland Soil, 148
22. Investigating Soils, 149
23. Measuring Acidity, 150

Ecological Issues in Woodland Soil Conservation, 152
24. How You Can Affect Deforestation Practices, 153
25. Identifying Environmental Stress, 154
26. Watch a Tree Grow, 156

Dry Zones

Deserts, Dunes, Sandlots, and Sidewalks, 157

Characteristics of the Area, 158
Common Inhabitants, 159

Survival in the Dry Zone, 163
1. Why Is It Dry?, 163
2. How Much Water Can the Soil Retain?, 165
3. Measuring Temperature Variations, 166
4. The Effects of Wind, 168

5. How Dry Zone Leaves Conserve Moisture, 170
6. Defense Tactics, 172
7. How Plants Affect the Dry Zone, 173
8. Look at a Cactus—But Not Too Closely!, 174
9. Animals That Live in the Dry Zone, 176

Endangered Desert Ecosystems, 178
10. How Can We Help Save Threatened Habitats?, 179

What Can Be Learned from Local Dry Zone Ecology?, 180
11. Our Dependence on Soil and Water, 180
12. How Can Soil Hold on to Water?, 181
13. Endangered Water Supplies, 182
14. What Can Be Done to Save Water Supplies? 184
15. Keeping Our Water Pure, 185

Bibliography, 187
Index, 191

Acknowledgments

This book was written as a way of continuing to teach while staying home with my young children. It has provided a great opportunity to compile and evaluate what I've gathered from my years of teaching and learning. As is true for many naturalists, my learning has come from the firsthand events of a life spent out-doors and from reading the accounts of nature writers and biologists.

The Bibliography at the back of this book lists the works of my favorite (and most accessible) writers. Other teachers were found at nature centers and schools and among students, friends, and family. I fondly, humbly acknowledge their gifts of information, patience, and criticism.

The writing of a book takes time. That it took my time is obvious, but it also took the time of my husband, David Longland, and of other friends who took care of my children while I worked. Tyler and Mollie are to be thanked for their willingness to be stopped and photographed when we came across suitable subjects for illustrations.

I want also to acknowledge the time given by my editors: Doe Boyle for her detailed consideration of the manuscript in its early stages, Laura Strom for her steady guidance and excellent sense of literary order and integrity, and my sister Marie Lynn Hunken (my first ecologist) for her help with the Dry Zone chapter.

All of these people wanted this book to happen, and because of their efforts it has.

Introduction

WHAT IS ECOLOGY?

When you look out the window or walk around outside, you can't see ecology. You see individual plants and animals, kinds of soils, clouds, or waterways. But those individuals are not ecology. Ecology is our understanding of how nature works as a whole. It is the study of living plants and animals that while breeding and birthing, consuming, growing, and decomposing, work like interlocking gears, passing a continuous flow of energy throughout the ecosystem. Ecologists look beyond individuals to these relationships—the habitual interactions of entire populations of plants and animals. Ecology, then, is the study of the Earth's beautiful machine, the ecosystem.

WHY LEARN ABOUT ECOSYSTEMS?

We live as part of the beautiful machine. The machine is alive and enormously complicated. The lives of every plant and animal are its workings, its systems. Where you live, what you eat, and how your wastes are distributed are your "home" system, your ecosystem. If you live in a desert among goat-herding people, you have a very different notion of your ecosystem than does a person from New York City. Your sense of personal responsibility is also different. Children of desert tribes know very well how resources must be used carefully. Most Americans live as though water, soil, and energy were unlimited.

We are finding out now that our relationship to our ecosystem must be modified. The clean water, clean air, abundant animal life, and fertile soils of North America have been poisoned and reduced by our wasteful activities. Now, both our large numbers and our shortsighted habits are endangering the quality of life we expect for ourselves and our children. Our new, improved "eco-logic," our ideas about our relationship to our environment, must be based on accurate knowledge and respect. Pollution is a natural process; in a balanced ecosystem, the wastes are recycled. We need to use those natural processes to keep our water drinkable, our clouds from poisoning trees and lakes, our farm soil more fertile with use, and a landscape alive with a huge, thriving variety of plants and animals.

HOW TO LEARN ABOUT YOUR ECOSYSTEM

You probably already have some habits that maintain your connection with your environment. Perhaps you enjoy nature programs on television or you read books about ecology or publications from environmental organizations you support. Perhaps you follow your community's recommendations on recycling wastes, or you make time to be outdoors. You will learn even more and feel more connected if you branch out to include new ways of participating. Activities such as teaching others, recording your observations, buying only recyclables, spending more quiet time in nature, and working to save undeveloped land will open in you a more complete awareness, a richer sense of connectedness to your own ecosystem. By learning more, you'll become a participant in nature who can evaluate present environmental situations and so influence events to come. A greater consciousness of the problems can be painful, but if the knowledge leads to action, there can be change.

HOW THIS BOOK CAN HELP YOU PARTICIPATE MORE FULLY

This book is about how natural systems operate in a variety of common North American habitats. The focus is on organisms whose relationships link them to a particular place. Each habitat chapter also includes typical examples of nutrient cycles, seasonal changes, and successional and historical events. An activity accompanies each example to encourage understanding, involvement, and curiosity. The humanmade problems that directly affect that habitat are also presented, along with suggestions for how to help solve the problems.

WHO WILL USE THIS BOOK

This book is a collection of nifty facts, ecological topics, and teaching activities for parents (working on a daily, intimate level with one or a few children), for leaders (teaching groups in a noncurricular situation such as scouting, camp, or other alternative educations), and for classroom teachers (teaching groups in a curriculum context, usually with an obligation to meet a variety of educational objectives such as grade levels in math, science, or history). Any activity can be modified to fit your circumstance. Parents may enjoy doing the activities a few at a time with a child; scout or camp leaders may want to take advantage of their opportunities to go outside; and classroom teachers may work activities into science or social studies curricula as appropriate and convenient. The habitat activities are presented sequentially, from basic observations to conceptual understanding, and can work as integrated curricula.

WHAT YOU CAN DO TO HELP MAKE A DIFFERENCE

This book has been developed and written in an effort to help people learn and encourage them to teach. By becoming an informed community activist, each person can help to change the attitudes and processes that are currently destroying our environment. The large environmental organizations still play important roles in lobbying and lawmaking, but they are often limited by their roles as deal-makers. Local activists have more power to take stands and to attract the attention of media. Gadflies can be more troublesome and effective than the bigshots who must be careful of their "public image." Learn locally, act locally, to heal globally.

USING THE HABITAT STUDY CHAPTERS

The activities and information that follow have been designed to help people of all ages learn about their environment, to become familiar with what is there, and to learn how it fits together in a system that includes people. The process of becoming familiar with any complicated system, such as understanding a sport, mastering a craft, or learning about a different culture, involves learning new terms that represent specific objects, events, and concepts and experiencing a new range of sensory perceptions. The smells, sounds, and sights of a familiar locale take on new meanings. As people gradually learn to distinguish and interpret events, they begin to anticipate what will happen next and begin to understand that we are all a part of a natural process.

To learn about ecology, one must learn ecologically—that is, by interacting with living systems. If a person only reads about ecosystems or watches television programs on nature, that person will still not know what is going on just outside the door. One must experience nature firsthand to know about the endangered plants, rare animals, and the little wildernesses all around us.

Whether you are a teacher, a student, or both, as you do the activities suggested in each habitat study chapter, please keep in mind these considerations:

- **Make the activity hands-on.** By handling the objects of study (where appropriate), your brain will absorb much more information; you may not be conscious of all that you learn, but the memory of the experience will help you make connections and perceive details at other times.

- **Use a variety of learning styles.** Holistic learning, involving all your information pathways, results in holistic understanding—a view of the whole picture. In your exploring process use combinations of measuring, descriptive writing, drawing, and finding analogies. Some approaches in this book may already be familiar; try all approaches so that new information is stored in many parts of your brain. A process that enhances creative problem-solving involves defining the problem to be solved and then finding the solution during activities such as dreaming, exercising, drawing, doodling, explaining to others, or performing some activity analogous to the problem. We are currently in great need of people who know a great deal about ecology and are creative problem-solvers.

- **Use learning activities that build understanding.** Since ecological concepts are about sequences and cycles, let your learning follow that pattern. When you are approaching a new ecosystem, start by finding out (1) *what is there* (what can be immediately observed?), then observe (2) *where is it found* (in what company and context does it occur?), and then consider (3) *what are the connections* (what else is it like? how is it different? how does it affect the other ecosystems?). By using that basic sequence as a cycle you will learn more. If you are teaching others, try to combine activities in units that reflect the what-where-how sequence.

The activities described in each habitat chapter are arranged to first familiarize you with the most obvious attributes of the study area and then to show you how those elements represent basic ecological concepts. You don't have to follow the sequence as written, but if you begin with one near the end of a chapter, read the preceding activities so you do not miss any introductory information.

HINTS FOR LEADERS

For every activity you will do best by responding to the interests of the children. Show enthusiasm for the objects children find or identify. Once they know that their findings and wonderings get them individual attention, they will explore in earnest to find more to show you.

A guide who knows the local natural history can be a magical help for beginners, but don't overwhelm. The best teachers connect the new information to previous experiences. To help learners feel empowered, let people know that you, too, are a learner, that the information you have comes from others.

People seem to learn easily when a session begins with quick-paced interactions. The high energy can then be applied to group or individual observations that can be used to help learners make connections. It is helpful to finish off with opportunities to express the experience. Whether you use this four-step pattern as a basis for a single excursion or a summer's curriculum, you will find that it helps people of all ages learn. Try to find (or create your own) activities that use this sequence:

Interacting: Start with activities that involve movement, games of fast-paced interaction between players, or short-term team competitions. (Avoid individual competitions.) These activities are especially helpful when working with children, for whom physical interaction is the primary mode for learning.

Observing: Once the senses have been enlivened by physical activity, the learner(s) can observe their surroundings more carefully. Young children might need to work as a group taking turns describing objects, but older learners can work alone. Writing and sketching can be used as collecting devices to bring observations back to the group.

Finding connections: Talk about what has been seen and find relationships, such as predator-prey relationships, growth stages, plant succession, and life cycles. Detailed examples and activities are included in the chapters on individual habitats.

Expressing Contributions: Give each person a chance to tell or show what he or she has found. Sharing gives value to personal observations and reminds everyone of what happened during the session. The activity can be as simple as asking each participant to name one thing noticed that day or as elaborate as a group's comparison of habitats. If possible, find examples in the work of artists and writers. Artists, poets, and ecologists are all in search of meaningful connections.

Backyard Ecology

AREAS OF HEAVY USE:

SCHOOL YARDS, SUBURBAN YARDS,

PLAYGROUNDS, AND PARKS

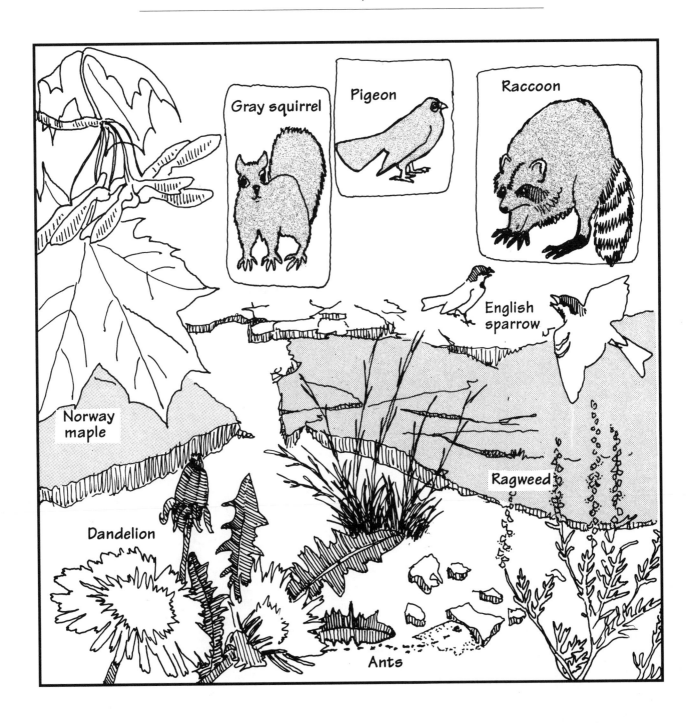

Characteristics of the Area

You can be an ecologist by studying habitats near people. Yards and gardens, playgrounds, city trees, and vacant lots have plenty of examples of natural processes at work. Ecosystems aren't found in just the wild and distant places. Every plant and animal that you see in your neighborhood has a role in the local ecosystem. If you carefully observe any one living thing, you can see that as it grows and reproduces and makes food (plants) or gets food (animals), it changes its environment. An ecosystem is like a very complicated weaving, in which the strands represent the interactions of the plants and animals. Each blooming, each feeding, each nesting, and even each death is an example of the way energy moves through the network of relationships; each act affects the lives of other organisms by creating or by limiting the conditions they need to live. The activities that follow will help you to learn from the plants and animals that are already able to make a living from the human habitat outside your door.

Common Inhabitants

The following plants and animals are commonly found in most of the urban and suburban habitats of North America. If the area you study does not have all of these species, look for similar species and relationships that might be there.

PLANTS	ANIMALS
Trees and Shrubs	Grey squirrel
Pin oak	Fox squirrel
Crabapple	Pigeon
Red cedar (a juniper)	Garter snake
Field juniper	Brown snake
Yew	Skunk
Ailanthus	Raccoon
Norway maple	Mole
Northern bush-honeysuckle	Vole (meadow mouse)
Blackberry	Starling
Raspberry	English sparrow (house sparrow)
	Earthworm
Herbaceous Plants	Yellow jacket
Little bluestem grass	Sowbug
Crab grass	Millipede
Dandelion	Centipede
Plantain	Woolly bear caterpillar
Burdock	Ant
Queen Anne's lace	Cicada
Lamb's-quarters	Bagworm
Ragweed	Japanese beetle

Relationships to Look for

Bagworms and junipers. Junipers are prickly leaved shrubs that are often used in a hedge or a foundation planting for homes or public buildings. They don't usually grow very tall, and their branches stretch out in a starburst shape. Juniper leaves have a pungent smell when rubbed; the fruit is a dry berry that turns from green to light blue when ripe. The caterpillars of a species of bagworm moth live in little drooping bags made of silk from glands under their mouths. The larva feed on the juniper leaves and, as they grow, enlarge their cases by adding more silk. The bags are well camouflaged with segments of juniper leaves woven into the outside. When the caterpillars reach their full size, they change into pupa, using their bags as cocoons. The female moths emerge wingless; the winged males seek out cases where the females wait. Eggs are laid inside the bag and later hatch from that safe place. After hatching, the young make their own bag homes and begin to eat the juniper leaves.

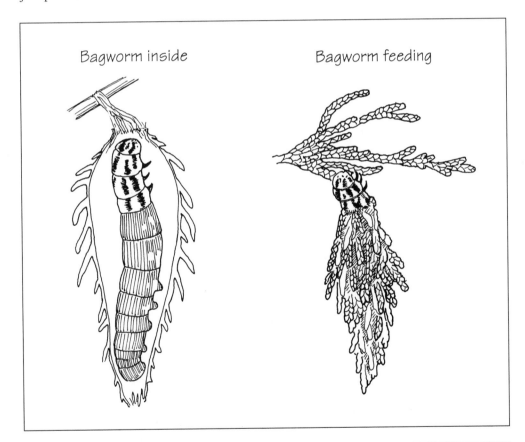

Bagworm inside   Bagworm feeding

HOW TO FIND BAGWORMS

Juniper plantings that are growing in dry open habitats such as parking lot borders are likely to have the most bagworms. Look along the underside of the branches for the cases. The leaves and stems that cover the case will probably be the reddish brown color of dead juniper. There are usually many bagworms on a single plant; once you find one, look for others. A bagworm that is still growing is easily removed from its position. Those in pupation (or old cases) will be strongly attached by silk strands. (Bagworms also live on other species of woody plants. Check arborvitae, locust, pine, and other ornamental trees and shrubs.)

Yellow jackets, caterpillars, and picnic food. Yellow jackets are common wasps, especially prevalent in late summer when their colonies have grown to large numbers of female workers. Throughout the summer months the workers are busy capturing soft-bodied insects (mainly caterpillars) to feed to the young yellow jackets, which live in a many-chamber paper nest, often built in an old chipmunk hole. The workers themselves keep fueled with nectar gathered from blossoms within their territory. Yellow jackets are in their hunting mode when slowly flying in search patterns, investigating the underside of leaves or along stems. When one worker finds a caterpillar, it kills the prey with bites. A large caterpillar will be sliced into manageable pieces and transported in sections. You can see yellow jackets working over open areas, such as walls, often pouncing on dark spots that they mistake for small insects.

In the early fall, the workers are still gathering protein and eating sweets, but things start to change when the queen yellow jacket dies. The queen keeps the workers organized through chemical messages, and with her death the colony begins to fall apart into random behaviors. Fermented fruit is also available at this time, and the combination of alcoholic juice and rowdy behavior turns yellow jackets into unpredictable hazards.

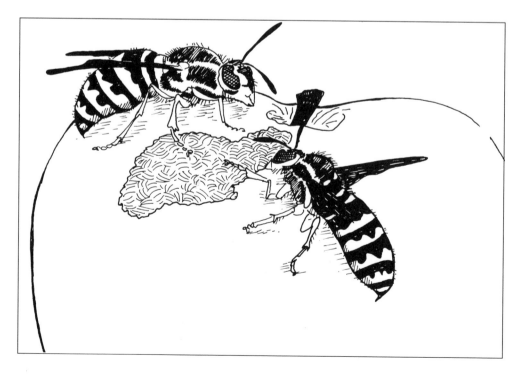

HOW TO FIND YELLOW JACKETS

Yellow jackets probably found you when you were trying to eat a sandwich outside in late summer. The workers are attracted to people food—the meaty odors of hot-dogs, hamburgers, and tunafish and the sweet smell of fruit juice and soda bring yellow jackets up very close. Yellow jackets are not likely to sting while hovering around your food. They definitely will sting, however, if you step on their nest hole. In late summer, the hunting wasp can be aggressive and intolerant. Rather than try to fight off a yellow jacket, set aside a small amount of whatever food she is after and observe her methods of shearing off portions of meat or lapping up juice. Look for interactions between yellow jackets as they jockey for feeding positions. (Also look for yellow jackets working over road kills and carrion. Although wasps are not officially in the category of "decomposers," they are certainly recyclers when it comes to turning dead meat into live yellow jackets.)

Cicadas and trees. When the hottest days of summer come, the trees begin to buzz with the drone of cicada song. The male cicadas make the song by vibrating special plates on their abdomens. The females are attracted by the sound to the male's location. After mating, the female lays a number of eggs in a slit she makes near the end of a tree twig. This often weakens the twig so that it breaks at the slit. (Look for a brown, dead cluster of leaves [often on oaks] as evidence of egg laying.) The tiny young hatch, fall to the ground, and burrow down to the roots. They have piercing and sucking mouthparts for extracting sap from the roots. This sap is their only food for their lifetime. The nymphs of the annual cicada are full grown by the following summer (unlike their long-lived relatives, the seventeen-year locusts), at which time they dig their way to the surface, using the large, front digger-claws that characterize their nymphal phase. Clumsy and vulnerable, the nymphs emerge on an evening, climb up the nearest tree trunk, and by morning have shed the brown nymph skin. The cicada is now a green-and-black adult with transparent wings and a liking for loud, monotonous singing.

HOW TO FIND CICADAS

Other than their sound, the best evidence of cicada time is cast-off nymph skins, usually found at kid-height on the trunk of a tree. Intact and still clinging to the bark, the skin looks like a whole creature. It is easily removed from the bark and can be carefully examined. You can distinguish the digger-clasper feet, the piercing mouthpart, and even the pair of bristly antennae. Try going out after dark during cicada time and checking the tree trunks for climbing nymphs. (They will wave those claws around a bit, but if held by their back, they cannot pinch.) Let them

finish their climb on the inside of your window screen. The winged adult may emerge before your bedtime, or it may not push out until dawn. Get up as early as you can to catch the cicada in its freshly hatched colors of pink and bright green. (The golden dots on its forehead, the ocelli, are found on many insects and spiders.)

Starlings and Japanese beetles. Starlings are common in city, suburbs, and farmland because short grass and pavement are their best habitats for finding food. You may notice flocks of these short-tailed birds soaring or large groups of them walking. They also appreciate the kinds of nesting and roosting opportunities offered by ledges on city buildings, school walkways, bridge understructures, and barns. One of their favorite foods is the larvae of Japanese beetles, which are abundant eaters of grass roots in parks, lawns, and pastures. Both of these animals were introduced to this country, and both have become pests by overpopulating and using resources needed by native creatures. (Diseases and predators on this continent were not adapted to these aliens.) The aliens are now very much a part of our landscape, and they still have lessons to teach us about how successfully introduced species can reduce the complexity and health of an ecosystem.

HOW TO FIND STARLINGS AND JAPANESE BEETLES

Starlings are ground-feeding, black-colored birds that walk (not hop) and have long, sharp bills and short tails. They eat both seeds and insects found by their probing bills. A feeding flock will commonly move in one direction across an open area, with members toward the rear flying forward periodically to get in front. The nonbreeding birds form large flocks and often roost together at nightfall in a noisy crowd. The starlings' winter plumage is irridescent black speckled with light dots, resembling stars.

Japanese beetles spend most of their lives in the ground as white larvae, or grubs. The grubs feed on the roots of grasses and other field plants. By midsummer they have pupated and emerged as bronze-and-green beetles with a great appetite for tender vegetation. The males are strongly attracted to the females; most clusters of feeding beetles also contain mating beetles. The scent, or pheromone, that the female uses to attract males has been synthesized and is available at hardware and garden centers. Even a small drop is a strong lure to males. With the commercial pheromone, you can set up experiments to find out what other clues attract the males. Experiment with pheromone on sheets of colored paper, on drawings of different-sized dots, or in various habitats to see which situations attract the most males.

Looking Carefully at What Lives Nearby

Whatever lives outside your doors has a name and has specific ways of interacting with both the physical conditions (temperatures, soil conditions, and weather changes) and the biotic conditions (other plants and animals) of the area. Your first step in learning about your local ecosystem is to find out what is there.

1 Keeping an Explorer's Journal

Materials:

- Writing materials (paper and pencil)

Background: Even without binoculars or a hand lens, the act of recording what you see brings whatever you are looking at into sharper focus and turns even a familiar area into a new world to be explored.

People have probably always been explorers of new land, eager to find new resources and to assess their possibilities. Written descriptions of the explorers' discoveries are both part of their evaluation process and a way to show others what they found. Early reports of the New World's plants and animals convinced European farmers, shipbuilders, trappers, and traders to come to America. Today they provide fascinating glimpses into the lost riches of our continent. (You might want to read some of the writings of John Smith, Governor William Bradford, the Bartrams, or Lewis and Clark. Some explorers also made maps or drawings. Look at the work of John White, who made observations of Virginia.)

Although the early documents were intended to encourage development, later writers, such as John Muir, wrote to convince people that special habitats should be preserved. These days, as our society is learning to value variety and protect complicated systems, detailed ecological studies are required by law before a natural area can be developed.

Procedure: Select some area to explore and describe. Decide first what aspects of the habitat you want to assess and for whom you are writing. Do you want to convince settlers to come? What special plants or animals live here? Perhaps you are writing for a travel agency that is trying to promote tourism of a scenic area or perhaps you are a real estate broker trying to sell a building lot. If the area has special attributes, describe them and write to convince others of the importance of protecting the ecosystem in which they exist.

Include in your description (1) the plants, animals, or geological qualities that are typical of your area, and (2) features that illustrate or symbolize your area's special qualities. Include pictures of some typical plants or animals in your final report.

2 Plant Places

Materials:

- Collecting bag
- Tree and wildflower identification books (a book especially for weed identification might be helpful)

Background: The main reason for describing the place is to distinguish the particular kinds of plants found in the area. Plants are so important because they are the primary source of energy in any ecosystem; they are the only organisms that are able to use sunlight to create food. The majority of all animals are plant eaters. Besides being used as food, plants are used for home-making, hiding, lookouts, and shelter. You will probably find that the greater the variety of plants in your area, the greater the variety of animals.

Procedure: Make a survey of all the species of plants found in your area. If you are working with others, you may want to divide up the area into manageable sections. Try to notice and perhaps write down any special characteristics of the place where you find each individual. Listing the names of plants is preferable to collecting specimens, but it is reasonable to do some collecting if you take only one leaf per species and work in small groups when there are lots of collectors. If you don't know plant

Plants that live in a field tend to have narrow leaves to reduce the effects of intense light (water loss in the plant), and plants that live under trees tend to have wider leaves to help them capture the limited sunlight.

names, just searching for the different shapes that distinguish plant species is an important learning process. *Do* learn the characteristics of any poisonous or rare plants in your area before you start. *Don't* take any leaves from endangered or rare plants or plants that have only a few leaves. Collect only from common plants or individuals with abundant leaves.

When you have your collection assembled, review your notes and drawings and try to remember how each plant looked and where it was growing. Pay attention to (or discuss with others) which plants were found together. Try to describe the characteristics of the place. Was it sunny? Shady? Wet? Did it have sandy soil? Rocky? Are there any similarities in the shapes of the leaves that remind you of where it was found?

3 Signs of Animals in Your Area

Materials:

- Notebook and pencil

Background: The area you are exploring may look deserted, but once you know the signs to watch for, and you begin to look for them, the evidence of activity, if not the animals themselves, will become visible to you.

Look for pathways: Most mammals will follow the same track when traveling to and from favorite feeding areas. Check for beaten paths on hill slopes, in the gaps in fences or walls, along the banks of streams, or along the grassy border of a field or clearing.

Look for tracks: Soft soil or sand along the edge of a pond or stream may hold footprints or the marks of bills or claws. Check the snow-covered ground, especially in late winter when the nonhibernators are out looking for food and mates. Check for scratches on trees made by climbing squirrels, raccoons, or by male deer rubbing their antlers.

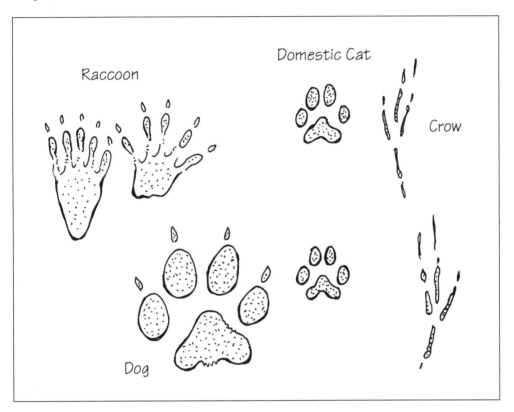

Look for signs of feeding: Squirrels and skunks dig shallow holes. Rabbits snip twigs cleanly like a scissors cut. Deer tear twigs, often leaving a strip of bark at the cut. Woodpeckers search for bark insects by prying off bark or chiseling out rotten wood (the round holes in upright wood are woodpecker homes). Mice and squirrels leave gnawed nutshells.

Look for digested food: Foxes and raccoons leave their droppings in prominent spots as territory markings. The ground under the favorite perches of hawks, owls, and herons is often marked by conspicuous white splashes. Owls and hawks cough up and drop dry pellets containing the hair, feathers, and bones of their prey. Deer leave small piles of pellets along paths; their winter pellets are woodier than the softer summer pellets.

Look for homes: Squirrels make large, rounded leaf nests in trees. Jays, crows, hawks, and owls build bulky, flat-topped nests close to the tree trunk. Woodpecker holes are also used by chickadees, titmice, flying squirrels, screech owls, and deer-mice. Large hollows in an upper trunk or limb might be the home of raccoons, opossums, wood ducks, or barred owls. Holes in the ground and/or mounds of fresh earth might indicate (in order of size and depending on where you live): ants, earthworms, tiger beetle larva, solitary bees, spider wasps, turret spiders, crayfish, shrews, voles, moles, chipmunks, gophers, ground squirrels, woodchucks, skunks, gopher tortoises, or foxes. Animals that do not dig but need the burrows of others include yellow jackets, snakes, and burrowing owls.

Procedure: Consider each of the categories listed above as an item in a treasure hunt. Try to find one example of each category in your area. Describe (and sketch, if possible) each item you find, using a format similar to the following:

Area:_____ Date:_____ Weather conditions:_____

Path: (Where found, what it looks like, possible identity of maker)

_____

_____

Tracks: (Where found, condition of surface, possible identity and activity)

_____

_____

Signs of feeding: (Where found, type of food, possible identity of animal)

_____

_____

Digested food: (Where found, general description, possible identity)

_____

_____

Animal home: (Where found, general description, possible identity)

_____

_____

Is the temperature the same in every part of your study area? Which areas might be warmer? Which might be cooler?

_____

_____

4 Small Seek

Materials:

- Hand lens (a plastic "bugbox" with a lens in the lid is ideal)

Background: Complete worlds of tiny creatures live in places we seldom see. You can find them once you know where to look.

Procedure: Look carefully in dark, moist places. Check under rocks, layers of leaves, loose bark on dead wood, under rocks near water, and under boards or logs that have been on the ground more than one week. _IMPORTANT:_ (1) Always put the covering material back in the same position you found it in. (2) Snakes, yellow jackets, and scorpions live in these places. If poisonous snakes live in your area, take special care to lift the corner of a log or rock farthest from you or roll the log toward you, so that an alarmed creature can move away from you to escape. If you are exploring in middle or late summer, when yellow jacket colonies are especially aggressive, spend a minute or two watching for the wasps that are moving in direct flight to and from the same place in the ground. Stay far away from the nest hole; they give no warning before launching a painful attack.

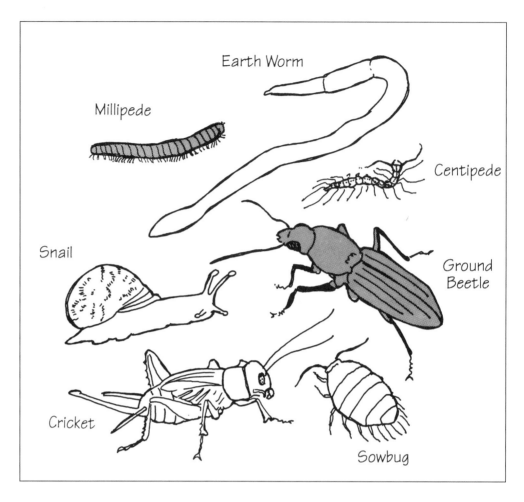

Look in moist, dark places for the following:

Pillbug: Grey, oblong creature with many segments and many legs; rolls up in a ball when picked up.

Sowbug: Similar to pillbug but doesn't roll up; has a "skirt" of grey "legs" dragging behind.

Centipede: Long body and many legs that stick out on either side of the body; moves rapidly. *Don't handle, they can bite.*

Millipede: Lots of short legs under a long, tubelike body; rolls up when disturbed.

Snail or slug eggs: Transluscent, slightly sticky whitish eggs, 1mm. (or $1/8$ of an inch) in diameter.

Spider eggs: A small cluster of eggs, covered with a white or brownish silk fabric.

Ants: Will rapidly try to move whatever they have stored in the place you've disturbed. Very tiny, round eggs. Larvae like tiny caterpillars, pupae (most likely to be found close to the surface) encased in cream-colored oblongs. During cold months you might find aphids in an ant chamber. In the spring, the ants will carry the aphids to a growing stem, protect them from predation, and "milk" them of their sweet secretions.

Salamanders: Predators of this underworld. Always wet your hand (on wet leaves, perhaps) before touching a salamander. Your dry skin can remove the protective slime on the salamander's skin, leaving the animal vulnerable to infection or abrasion.

Earthworms: Long pink worms with a slightly thicker band of skin near the head end. The ring is the site where genetic material is exchanged during mating. Fertile eggs will later be laid by *both* individuals.

Ground beetles: Fast shiny black beetles

Mycellium: White or orange threads, branching and slightly elastic; these are the food-getting strands of mushroom plants. The mushrooms that grow above-ground are the spore-producing part of the whole plant. Mushroom mycellium from a single plant may weave through acres of soil.

Spiders: The ground-living funnel-weavers make dense, sheetlike webs; a webless spider that hurries away is probably a wolf spider. Females may be carrying a white ball of eggs or a dense cluster of babies on their bodies.

Slugs: Slimy, muscular oblongs; look on one side for a "porthole" that is used for breathing; snails have similar body shapes but carry shells and live in soils that have lime in them.

Describe and draw the creatures you find as you explore the habitat of darkness and moist soil.

5 Choosing a Personal Habitat

Materials:

- Notebook and pencil

Background: As you explore your outdoor area, you may find that in some areas you feel more comfortable than you feel in others. It seems to be a part of human nature to respond differently to different habitats. That reaction often reflects other experiences we have had with similar places. These emotional responses of comfort or uneasiness are very much a part of our relationship to our environment. Explore your own feelings by searching for your own special place and exploring what you find there.

Procedure: Find a place to sit where you can comfortably observe an area that interests you. Spend some time looking around and getting to know what is there. Imagine being a small, inquisitive creature exploring every rock, tree, and tuft of grass. After your initial explorations, use the following questions to sharpen your awareness.

- Describe the surface of where you are sitting.

- Look up to the sky. If there are any objects (such as branches or a building) between you and the sky, describe what it is and how it affects your area (including you).

- When you look out over the area, what do you see? Describe the landscape—colors, textures, groups of plants, geological features, and creatures.

- What sounds do you hear? Are some constant? Are some intermittent?

- What odors do you notice? Where are they coming from?

- When you look around, does any part of your view have a greater abundance of plants and animals? Describe the general view of two directions.

- During the time you have spent in your place, has any one plant or animal become particularly special to you? Describe it.

Wear and Repair—The Interactions of People, Plants, Creatures, and the Elements

The areas near human habitats are full of examples of the overuse of land and the undiversification of plants. But each place that shows wear also shows life on the rebound. Where soils are compacted and eroded, plants and animals that specialize in such habitats are trying to grow and live. Where plants are mowed, weeded, and restricted, other plants are finding a niche that suits them. Garden soils grow weeds, and cultivated same-species plantings attract abundant pests. Many of the natural processes that people try to overcome are events that lead to variety and complexity, the basis of a healthy ecosystem.

6 Hard Land, Soft Land

Materials:

- Paper for recording information and for making a map
- Pencils; perhaps colored markers

Background: The land near public buildings or suburban lawns is often heavily used by people. The grassy spots where people frequently walk or sit become worn and hard. Begin exploring at the most worn-out, bare section of soil you can

find: the path to a play area, a shortcut across a grassy section, or the edge of a
paved sidewalk.

Procedure: You can sense the different densities of soil by standing on your tiptoes
and then dropping down to a flat-foot stance. The jolt of that small drop will feel
stronger on a compacted pathway than on a lawn. Compare the jolt of a pavement
with that of compacted soil. A difference can also be felt by pushing a pencil point
into different densities of soil. The results will vary with the strength of the person,
but each can feel the difference. Try the softer zone first, marking the depth on the
pencil with tape or a rubber band; push the pencil into the compacted zone next,
and then record the results. Use both the heel-drop test and the pencil-pushing test
to find out where the hard soil and soft soil zones are in your study area. Record
your findings on a rough map of the area.

Why is Compacted Soil Hard on Plants?

Think about the reasons why walking on the ground would kill plants. It is obvious
that the trampling breaks the leaves and stems of the plants, but it may not be
immediately obvious that long-term damage is being done when the soil is compacted. In compacted soil, the particles that make up the soil are pressed together.
Not only is the soil physically harder, but without air spaces, a root cannot grow or
even breathe. After a rain, air spaces in uncompacted soils fill with water the same
way that spaces in a sponge hold water. These many tiny reservoirs provide moisture for nearby roots as well as for the fungus and bacteria that live in healthy soil.

7 Soil on the Run

Materials:

- Two 5-inch containers with holes in the bottom
- Soil
- Sod (chunk of soil with grass roots)
- Water
- 2 clear containers

Background: You may notice that most paths and worn zones are lower than the surrounding soil level, especially on slopes. Although the compression of many footfalls lowers the soil level (like a sponge when squished), some of the missing soil has been carried away by rain runoff and wind. The higher soil outside the worn zone is held in place by a netlike weaving of the root-growing plants. Even their leaves help hold soil by blocking the scouring forces of wind and rain. Once the plants are gone, however, the protection to the soil is gone, and erosion can take the soil away.

The soil in a pathway may be so tightly compressed that there is no room for roots and no spaces for the water and air. Plantain roots are adapted for compacted conditions by having two kinds of roots: thin moisture-collecting roots and thick compaction-breaking roots.

Procedure: You can experiment with the erosion-stopping power of plant roots by creating your own models. Two containers with perforated bottoms (see photo) can hold your samples—a sample of loose soil and a piece of lawn or field sod, freshly dug. (If you have only one container, it can be used for both samples, one at a time.) Hold each container at a slant and pour a set amount of water over each sample. Retain the water runoff in a clear container for each sample. Compare the samples and think about what happened. Which runoff sample had the most soil in it? Which soil sample retained the most moisture? If the samples represented large fields and a whole day of rain, what would a nearby stream look like? What would the fields look like? Which field would support the lives of the most creatures (including people)?

Lost Riches: What Erosion Takes Away

Soils of grassy areas are usually darker with more leafy bits mixed in than the gritty, sandy soils of the path. This is the "good stuff," the mix of organic bits and mineral particles that hold the rich supply of nutrients that plants need for growth. If there is no protective network of roots and leaves to hold the topsoil in place, this natural resource will be eroded by wind and water.

8 Be an Erosion Detective

Materials:

- Notebook and pencil
- A copy of this activity

Procedure: Not all erosion is the result of overused land. Wind and rain also erode the environment. Look for signs of erosion in the neighborhood.

Try to find two examples of each of the following. Record your observations.

- Rocks on a slope that are larger than sand-size and sticking up above the surface. Rain or wind has probably taken the smaller particles away, leaving these rocks exposed.

  _____

  _____

- Cement and asphalt. The harder pieces of a paving mixture, such as stones in a cement mix, are more resistant to wear. Compare flat and sloping portions of paved areas, looking for some of the harder ingredients that appear to be raised on the eroded parts.

  _____

  _____

- Rock outcrops and the corners of stone and brick buildings. Check for the smoothing action of wind or water erosion. Individual stones might be smooth all over, an indication of earlier erosion caused by running water or wave action.

  _____

  _____

9 Excavators in the Ecosystem

Materials:

- Notebook and pencil

Background: Even while people-feet erode and compact the earth, other organisms are reversing the damage. During the night earthworms back out of their tunnels and deposit little globs of soil that they have eaten at the surface and while tunneling. Ants pile granular particles around an open hole. Moles, gophers, and woodchucks open up networks of tunnels and push piles of earth to the surface.

All these tunnels modify the effects of compaction by opening spaces for air and moisture. They also increase the fertility of the surface soil. Mineral nutrients can be carried out of reach of shallow-rooted plants when they are dissolved in downward seeping rainwater. Burrowing creatures excavating in the deep soils bring them back to the surface.

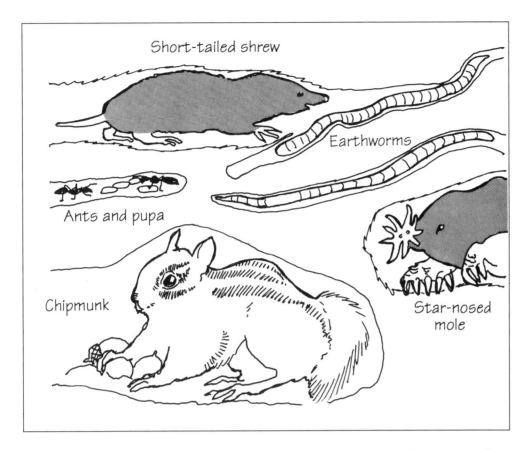

Short-tailed shrew

Earthworms

Ants and pupa

Chipmunk

Star-nosed mole

Procedure: Search your area for signs of tunneling by ants and earthworms on the surface of the soil. Evidence of excavations will be more visible in the mornings before they dry out or become trampled.

10 Cashing in on the Riches of Disturbed Soil

Materials:

- A Queen Anne's lace plant with a flowering stalk
- A Queen Anne's lace plant without a flowering stalk

Background: Humans take on the role of burrowing creatures when they dig holes or shovel up the ground to make a garden. By disturbing the soil, we create air spaces and bring nutrients to a level where seedling plants can use them. You may notice that plants along the edges of a dirt path tend to grow a little larger than the same species of plants growing farther from the path. By growing on the edge of a compacted area, the plants have access to the nutrients that erode from the compacted area.

Many of the plants of the pathside and abandoned fields have evolved a strategy for using disturbed soil situations. During the seedling's first growing season, it sends down a thick root and creates a cluster of leaves low to the ground. By the fall, most of the sugars that the leaves have made are stored as dense starch in the roots. When the warm weather returns the following spring, the plant converts this stored starch to sugars and rapidly sends up a tall flower stalk. After flowering and producing seeds, the entire plant dies.

Another characteristic of these "two-year," or biennial, plants is the making of many small seeds. The seeds are often equipped with rough or prickly seed coverings that may catch in the fur of an animal as it brushes by the pathside plant. This hitchhiking technique leads directly to reseeding, since the seed is likely to be dropped later along some other path or, if the carrier is a burrower like a fox, woodchuck, or skunk, the seed might be chewed out at the animal's doorstep—a freshly disturbed mound of earth.

Many of our root vegetables are varieties of biennial plants that have been selected for the sweetness and nutritional value of their first-year roots. Carrots, turnips, parsnips, and beets are a few biennial crops. (Try growing one of the mature roots in a garden over a summer season. The planted roots will send out leaves and a flower stalk and then produce seeds and die.) You can probably find wild carrots, or Queen Anne's lace, growing in the fields and playground borders of your neighborhood. The leaves look like the lacy carrot leaves of the garden vegetable; they are, in fact, the same species of plant, with the scientific name, *Daucus carota*. The wild plant represents the undeveloped variety that fits into the natural ecosystem. The garden variety has been "evolved" by growers who selected seeds from those plants that tasted good to people. Somewhere along the way their fur-catching seed coat was lost.

Procedure: You can observe some of the characteristics of wild biennials by digging up several Queen Anne's lace plants. (Although they are not native North American plants, Queen Anne's lace has existed near human habitats for a long time. The plant probably originated in an Asian ecosystem.) Your findings will depend on the season, but try to answer the following questions by looking at actual plants:

- Find a first-year Queen Anne's lace plant that is still only a clump (called a rosette) of leaves and a second-year plant that has a flower stalk. Which plant has the most lower leaves?

- Dig up and compare the root system of a first- and second-year plant. What differences do you see? Which has more stored food?

- In what ways does the wild plant resemble a carrot? Does it smell like a carrot? You can taste the root, but be ready for a bitter flavor. How might the bitterness benefit the wild-growing plant?

- Describe the flower, if it has any. (The flower disk is actually a cluster of tiny blossoms, each capable of making a separate seed.) If your flower cluster has a purple blossom in its center, try to figure out in what way that dark dot might help the plant. (No one knows, for sure.)

- If there are no seeds at the time, come back in late summer to see the "nest" of furry seeds. They have a pleasant, spicy smell and can be used to flavor sugar cookies. Remove the seed fur by rubbing the seeds between both hands or within a colander.

First year rosette on left, second year flowering stalk on right.

Changes in the Neighborhood Ecosystem

Plants are indicators of past and present environments. The plants that are able to grow in the worn zone are likely to be species that can cope with compact soil and physical stress. If the causes of compaction and erosion are reduced (perhaps a swing set is removed, a fence is put up, or steps are made on an eroded slope), the hardy plant species soon sprout in the bare spots. As these plants grow and die, their roots loosen the soil and their leaves add nutrients as they decay. Eventually, they create an environment for the next group of plants to sprout and grow.

Search around your study area and locate all the sites where hardy species are growing. Most of them are characterized by thick, wide leaves, often growing in a flat mound or rosette pattern. The hardiest grassy types usually grow in dense clumps. Places where the hardy colonizers grow along with grassy plants are either

Crab grass stretches its stems into a bare soil area. Roots may grow from the stem.

areas where the grasses are moving in, taking advantage of the loosened soil created by the hardy plants' roots, or where the soil has been disturbed within the grassy zone by burrowing animals such as moles, chipmunks, gophers, ground squirrels, or woodchucks.

11 Succession in the Backyard

Materials:

- Paper for survey notes
- Paper for writing or drawing
- Pencils (and markers if making drawings)

Background: How do you think your lawn would look if no one mowed it for a whole summer? You can probably imagine the grass getting long. It might even get long enough to move in the breeze; it would probably flower and make seeds. Unmowed grass tends to form clumps of individual plants instead of spreading out by means of its underground stems called tillers. Letting grass grow long also removes the broadleaved lawn plants such as dandelions and plantains, which are shaded by the tall grass and therefore killed.

If you can fence off just a portion of a mowed lawn, including a worn patch where hardy weed plants are already seeding in, you might get a chance to see the succession of different groups of plants growing one after another. If you watch the worn area, you will first see the hardy pioneers—the plantains, dandelions, or mustards—grow, flower, and set seeds. (The species of pioneer plants will vary with locale.) As the wide weed leaves and tough roots change the growing conditions, grasses will move in, eventually overwhelming the pioneers.

What do you think would happen next? Do you see any examples in your neighborhood of plants that grow up out of unmowed grass areas? Many kinds of trees and shrubs specialize in growing in grass habitat. One characteristic habit is the production of seeds that can be carried by wind. Maples, ashes, poplars, ailanthus, and pines grow well in sunny areas and seed readily among grasses. Seeds innocently "planted" by birds may produce shrubs such as sumac, rose, and elderberry.

By the time this group of trees and shrubs has matured into fully grown plants, the lawn grass is long gone and the land becomes woods. In most parts of North America, succession includes one more facet—species of trees from seeds that can sprout in moist soils and grow in the shade. Oaks, hickories, beech, and some kinds of evergreen trees usually make up this last group. These trees are succession's finale, but their growth does not signify the end of change. Eventually, a windstorm, fire, drought, or bulldozer will disturb the ecosystem and the land will start again with whatever nearby plant seeds are available to grow in the conditions at hand.

Procedure: Look for examples of each stage of plant succession in your neighborhood in places that are not mowed. You need to find (1) pioneer plants, (2) grass and tall wildflowers, (3) trees and shrubs that create the transition from field to woodland (look especially for producers of wind-blown and bird-eaten seeds), and (4) shady woodland species. Make up a future sequence of events for a worn area that you know. Start by describing the worn spot and how it became that way, and then create a description (or a drawing) of each stage of successive change, using the plants from your survey. Include creatures that might be found among the particular plants.

Neighborhood Trees Under Stress

Trees that live in the city or near streets are more likely to be affected by to root damage or pollution of air or soil. Frequently, a stressed tree will be vulnerable to diseases or insect infestations that a healthy tree is able to resist. Stressed broad-leaved trees are also more likely to change color and lose their leaves earlier in the fall than will healthier trees of the same species. Trees that are newly planted or recently stressed by construction activities will also show early color.

12 Berry Bush "Strategies"

Materials:

- A variety of berries (store-bought berries can be used if fresh)

Many berry plants have grown up in the protection of this juniper shrub. Deadly nightshade can be seen. A chokecherry tree may eventually shade out the juniper altogether.

Background: You may find that many of the plants that grow beneath trees and shrubs produce berries as seeds. Blackberries, honeysuckle, deadly nightshade, cherries, wild crabapple, bittersweet, and roses are examples of common berry plants that take advantage of the good growing conditions under woody plants. Berry plants have fleshy fruit that usually turn red or darken when ripe (although some are white-fruited). Often their stems are vines or fast-growing wood. Their methods of dispersing seeds is also characteristic. Many berries are eaten by birds, which then may roost in the branches of a tree or shrub. After a bird digests the fleshy part, the hard, inner seed passes out of the body to the soil below. The moist leaf litter is an ideal seedbed for a young sprout. A vine or cane is a good adaptation for a plant that often sprouts in the shade but needs sunshine for optimal growth. A cane or vine can stretch past its shady starting place, outgrowing both the nursery shrub and any nearby grasses.

Procedure: Collect a variety of berries in various stages of ripeness. Describe any distinctive characteristics (color, juiciness, texture, seeds) and try to identify any attributes that might help the plant adapt to its environment. Note any animals that might help spread the fruit. CAUTION: DO NOT TASTE ANY WILD BERRY unless

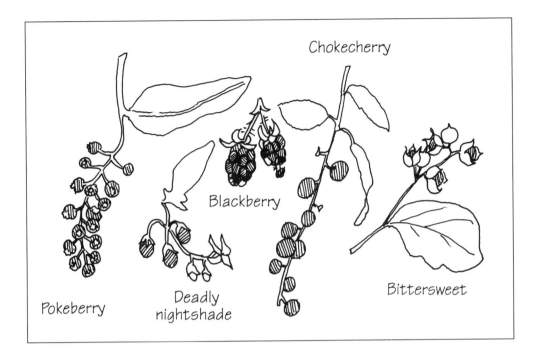

you are certain of its identity. Some berries are poisonous to humans but not to birds. Be sure that even edible berries have not been chemically sprayed.

13 The House That Nature Built

Materials:

- Writing or drawing materials

Background: Like each verse of the story of the house that Jack built, each event you can think of leading to the growth of any given berry bush is a link in a chain. Each link represents a requirement of berry plant existence—past, present, and future. There are links that make a chain of events leading to the makeup of the soil, the weather conditions of the locale, the varieties of birds found in the neighborhood, the histories of introduced plants, and the ways people have used the land. Any break in that chain—for instance, the loss of a berry-eating species such as the robin—would jeopardize the berry's ability to reproduce.

Procedure: Choose one particular plant that you know about (or can learn about). Make a list, either written or drawn, of as many lives that connect to your plant as you can think of or find. It will probably be easiest to represent your information in the form of a flow chart, in which the plant is written in the center and its connecting links are written in lines radiating out from the center (see the illustration on the next page).

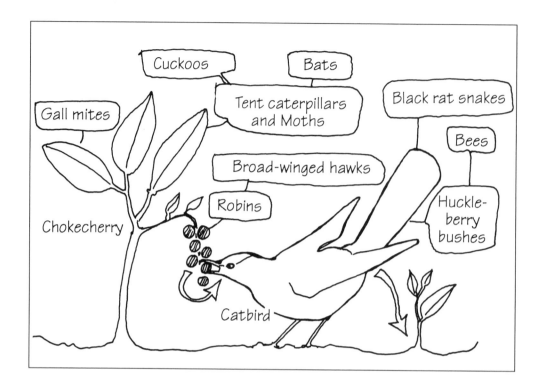

Gall mites

Cuckoos

Bats

Tent caterpillars
and Moths

Black rat snakes

Broad-winged hawks

Bees

Robins

Chokecherry

Huckle-
berry
bushes

Catbird

Litter

Somewhere along the edges of your study area the land will not be so heavily used.
Perhaps weeds or shrubs grow thickly or a fence keeps people from passing
through. The litter of leaves might be thicker here, blown into corners by the wind
or allowed to accumulate. This layer of organic material will probably be where the
most creatures live, hidden and protected by the denser vegetation. This may also
be where you find pieces of trash and inorganic objects. Trash can also provide
homes, but it can cause problems, too.

14 Analyzing Natural Leaf Litter

Materials:

- At least four pieces of light-colored paper
- Collecting bags

Background: The soil underneath a shrub has qualities that make it different from
the soils of both the grassy lawn and the worn zone. Carefully move aside the top
layers of leaves and twigs. You should be able to distinguish the seasonal layering of
each autumn's fall of leaves. Last year's leaves will be bright brown and still whole;

the leaves of the previous year will be duller and in smaller pieces; the older leaves will be increasingly chewed and rotted until you reach a layer where the gritty soil particles are mixed evenly with small pieces of decayed plants and animals.

Procedure: Take several scoopfuls of soil from each layer and spread the material out on pieces of light-colored paper. Which layer supports the largest community of roots and soil animals?

Sort materials found in the leaf litter according to readiness to break down into soil. Try to identify the various species of plants by their parts. Find fresh leaves that match the kinds of plants you found in the litter. Close the samples in clear, plastic bags (ones that have been used once already, please) and observe the decay process for several weeks. Include several examples of any trash you found for comparison.

The creation and subsequent breakdown of leaves is an essential natural cycle. All organisms in an ecosystem fit somewhere into that cycle: plants use recycled nutrients, and animals use plants. Our unrottable trash represents our attempts to slow down the recycling process, but having longer use of things has created new problems for ourselves.

15 Evidence of the Human Litterbug

Materials:

- Samples of trash litter found in your area (include pieces of foil, plastic, and paper products)

Background: If your study area is visited by numbers of people, you probably found evidence of another animal's lifestyle: the human litterbug. Look carefully at the human litter you find. What materials show the effects of decay or the breakdown of elements?

Procedure: Take pieces of materials that are commonly thrown away (aluminum foil, bag plastic, milk carton, newspaper, wax paper, or cardboard) and attempt to "get rid" of them. Weigh them first and then try to destroy them or reduce their amount. Think about any techniques you know of and try shredding, dissolving in water, rotting in a dark, moist place, and exposure to sunlight. Burning might seem like a good method for reducing mass, but it creates air pollution. Weigh and compare the results. Find out about the differences in the manufacturing processes of materials that break down readily and those that resist decay.

16 The Unrottables and the Rottables

Materials:

- Two same-sized jars, one with a lid
- Two pieces of toasted bread

Background: Paper, plastic, and metal cans are visible in most human habitats, and unless they are picked up and disposed of, they stay visible for a long time. Even when thrown "away," they take up space and cause pollution. Most of the stuff we buy cannot decay, and many products are never meant to be repaired. The result is a short-term life in the home and long-term existence in the landfill. Plastic packages do not decay, and even the paper parts of some packages are reinforced with plastic films. By comparison, flies, soil creatures, and the fungus and bacteria that live in leaf litter are able to reduce and recycle most plant and animal materials, so long as there is oxygen and moisture. If you are able to get permission to do so safely, explore an old surface dumpsite made in the early decades of this century. You might find glass and pottery pieces unchanged and perhaps a still-recognizable piece of boot leather or a rusty tractor part. But most of the litter in those years was organic and has decayed. Recent investigations into a trash dump made in the

1950s indicate that deep in the dry, oxygenless depths of a landfill waste food and paper products are unchanged, protected from decay.

Procedure: To get some idea of the role of oxygen and moisture as assets of decay, get two same-sized glass jars, one with a tight-fitting top. Put a piece of freshly toasted bread in each, close the lid on one jar, and observe the results for a week or more. The closed jar simulates a landfill situation where decay is inhibited by lack of oxygen and moisture.

17 The Compost Pile—Nature's Recycling System

Materials:

- Kitchen and yard waste (no inorganic materials)
- Six-foot section of chicken-wire fencing
- Loose soil

Background: The recycling process in a natural ecosystem is carried out by the soil creatures you can see and by millions of microscopic fungi and bacteria you cannot see. You can create a habitat for them and observe their recycling process by making a compost pile. Over two warm months, soil organisms can change organic garbage into rich soil.

Compost making can take a variety of forms. It can be a shaded heap of material, a pile contained by a wire fence, or a barrel with a lid to keep out dogs or raccoons. The barrel is open at the bottom and raised so finished compost can be scooped out.

Procedure: Make a compost pile outdoors for all your plant wastes. Curl a 6-foot or longer piece of chicken-wire fencing into a tube, bending the wire ends so they hold the fencing in a tube that can easily be loosened. (You'll need to unhook the tube to get at the finished compost.) Add any plant products to the pile: grass, leaves, vegetables, fruits, old bouquets. Let rooted weeds and grass dry out and die before adding them to the pile or you'll have a highrise grass garden. Avoid woody bits (they take too long to decompose) and meat, egg, and dairy scraps (they attract raccoons, rats, or other animals). You'll be impressed at just how much plant material you throw away and how great your composted soil looks. Add an inch-deep layer of loose soil for every foot of leafy stuff, if possible, to introduce soil organisms to the pile. Start a second pile when the first one is filled. Perhaps you can just take the wire off the first pile as it composts down. (Your pile will be only half as high as it was originally when the composting is finished.)

18 Eco-nomics: Buying into Recycling

Background: Most communities in North America must reduce the amount of waste they generate. It may not seem like a problem to an individual who puts out only a bag or two on trash collection day, but consider these statistics (compiled in 1988 by the Environmental Defense Fund):

- Every two weeks North Americans throw away enough glass containers to fill the twin skyscrapers of New York's World Trade Center.

- Every three months, we throw away enough aluminum containers to completely rebuild all our commercial airplanes.

- If all the iron and steel we throw away could be recycled, it would keep all the nation's automakers in continuous supply.

- Every year we throw away 24 million tons of leaves and grass clippings, precious (and free) soil nutrients that lie undecayed in our landfills.

- Every year we could build a wall of thrown-away writing paper 12 feet high— from Los Angeles to New York City.

- Every hour, we use 2.5 million plastic bottles, recycling only a small percentage.

All this adds up to mountains of discarded materials; mountains of processed resources put aside, out of reach, and, eventually, in our way. The best news is that people are able to do something about this problem. People are able to put pressure on government officials to make laws and restrictions that encourage recycling of materials. Industries are being required to take back and reuse their packaging. When communities make large amounts of presorted trash available, industries that recycle materials can become profitable. More people are selecting products on the basis of their ease of recycling their materials, and letting the store managers know that they are. As a result, the stores are putting pressure on distributors to get into the recycling line.

Procedure: Learn which materials are recyclable in your community and then buy accordingly. By buying packaging and products that are degradable or recyclable, you are exerting pressure on the stores and producers to do a better job, especially if you tell them what you are doing. Take advantage of any opportunities available to you for recycling, at recycling centers, at trash pickup, and at stores that offer to take back bags or bottles. Several books, which are listed in the Bibliography, offer good suggestions for reducing waste and setting up recycling systems. The following specific ideas can be acted on right away:

- Buy milk and juice in plastic instead of paper cartons. The paper cartons are plastic-coated and very difficult to recycle. The whitish plastic jugs, usually marked on the bottom with a number 2 inside a triangle, are usually accepted at community recycling centers.

- Ask your local sanitation department workers or recycling committee members to help devise a plan for recycling your school's writing paper and lunchroom trash. The first steps are always made by concerned individuals like you.

- Those handy little juice boxes, called asceptic cartons, have great potential in saving energy in transporting fresh juice. They have to go through special processes to be recycled, however, so it is better to use glass, #2 plastic, aluminum cans, or your own reusable container until you can find a place to recycle the juice box cartons.

- Choosing between plastic and paper bags in the supermarket can be tricky. Plastic bags take less energy to make than paper and can be recycled. Paper is biodegradable and can also be recycled into other paper products. Try to recycle the plastic (ask your supermarket to set up a pickup station) and use the paper bags at home for trash storage. (Do not be confused by "biodegradable" plastic trash bags that allegedly "break down." They eventually break down into tiny pieces, but they are still pieces of plastic. Because of their weakness, they cannot be used in plastic precycling processes.)

- Use cloth napkins and dishtowels as often as possible instead of paper products. "Recycled" toilet paper sounds offensive, but it is not. Most recycled paper products are made from scraps from the manufacturing process, not from used materials.

- Buy products that say "recycled," "nontoxic," or "biodegradable" as often as possible, even if they are a little more expensive. The purchases you make send messages to industries; the more we choose those labels, the more industries will respond. It might cost us more to make our environment healthier. Read labels carefully and pay attention to news stories about the authenticity of "green label" goods. Some people may be trying to cash in on the "ecology" market dishonestly.

- Precycle whenever possible. Don't buy products that come with lots of packaging (ten cents of your dollar goes for packaging, anyway). Choose recyclable containers; say "no, thanks" to bags when you don't need them.

- Learn to be a litter-grabber. Bend over and pick up that glass or trash in the grass.

- Put a stop to the constant flow of promotion material that comes through the mail. Write to the following address and tell them to take your name off the marketing list: Mail Preference Service, Direct Marketing Association, 11 West 42nd Street, P.O. Box 3861, New York, NY 10163-3861.

- Take extra but useable clothing, toys, and household articles to your local thrift store. Some secondhand clothing stores will give you money for items they can resell. While you're there, look around for recycled articles you can buy—this time you don't have to deal with expensive packaging!

Water Systems

STILL OR MOVING WATER:

PONDS, LAKES, BROOKS,

RIVERS, AND CREEKS

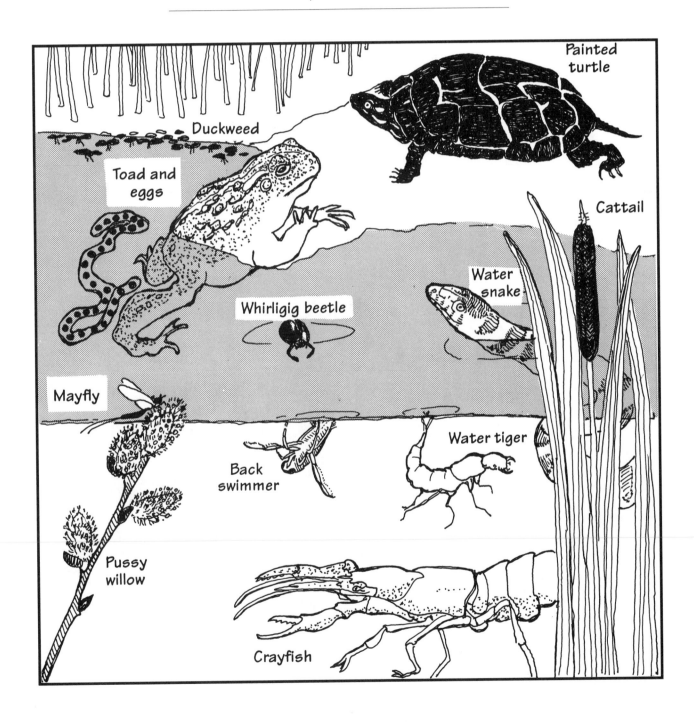

Painted turtle

Duckweed

Toad and eggs

Cattail

Water snake

Whirligig beetle

Mayfly

Water tiger

Back swimmer

Pussy willow

Crayfish

ater is essential to every living organism. Inside a plant or animal, water gives living tissue its shape and firmness. As sap or as a body fluid, water transports sugars and nutrients and takes away wastes. When moving in the environment, water carries particles, soluble minerals and chemicals, and heat. In this role as cleanser, water systems both transport and concentrate the materials that can be poisonous. In a balanced ecosystem the potential poisons are accommodated; mineral salts become part of another system (salt water) and wastes become nutrients for life forms downstream. By studying water ecosystems we can observe the processes, adaptations, and cycles that maintain them and we can understand how some of our human activities threaten to destroy that balance.

This chapter divides water ecology into two habitats: flowing water and still water. You may find that a brook with pools offers you both habitats or you may find that a slow-moving creek is more like a pond environment. Some of the organisms listed in one habitat may be found in both, and many of the conditions and problems apply to both habitats. The problems involving pollution from runoff and dumping follow the section on moving water, and the problems of acid precipitation follow the still water section.

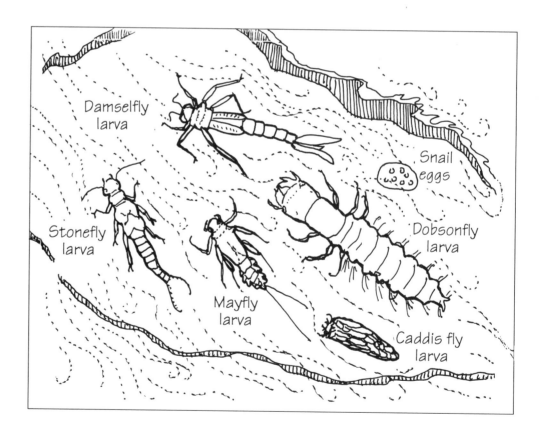

STREAMS—WATER ON THE MOVE

Characteristics of the Area

Flowing water and its specially adapted life forms may be found in many places. Irrigation drainage ditches, a shallow creek through a suburban park, or large rivers can all be explored using the following activities.

IMPORTANT: Do not drink from any brook, river, or pond. There is no such thing as pure surface water. Even clear mountain streams can carry bacteria that can cause long-term intestinal problems. Any water you are planning to ingest should first be boiled for twenty minutes.

Common Inhabitants

The following plants and animals are commonly found in most of the pond or stream habitats of North America. If the area you study does not have all of these species, look for similar species and relationships that might be there.

PLANTS	ANIMALS
Duckweed (ponds only)	Toad, tadpole
Skunk cabbage (streams only)	Frog
Moss and liverwort	Heron
Swamp loosestrife	Black fly larva (streams)
Willow	Grackle
Podomogetan	Mosquito
Bladderwort (ponds only)	Painted turtle
Red maple	Dragonfly and damselfly
Cattail (ponds only)	Sunfish (ponds only)
	Water snake
	Snail
	Water strider
	Whirligig beetle
	Freshwater mussel
	Stonefly and mayfly larva
	Salamander
	Crayfish
	Raccoon
	Dace and other minnows

Relationships to Look for

Red eft and red-spotted newt. The red eft is a small, bright orange salamander with short, rubbery limbs that can be found wandering across a woodland path after a rain. The red-spotted newt is a larger, softer creature of stillwater ponds. Its skin is a froggy green-brown, and it moves through the water by wagging its flat-finned tail. These seemingly different creatures are stages in the life of the same animal. The red eft is the land-walking form of the species. It leaves its pond birthplace and travels around feeding on small soil creatures. Eventually it returns to a pond, where it matures into the adult newt. This water form feeds on aquatic animals and is able to breed and lay eggs. By spending time in two different habitats, each individual uses a wide range of resources without the problem of adults competing for food with offspring. The expanded range is also an important factor for a creature that depends on shallow pools that may disappear with drought. The more vulnerable land stage is apparently distasteful to predators; its orange warning coloration even offers some safety to other salamander species that have chanced to evolve orange skin pigments.

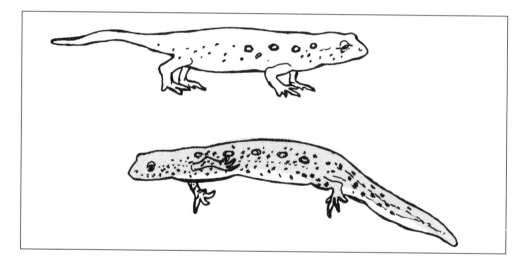

HOW TO FIND EFTS AND NEWTS

Efts keep to moist places. In the mornings or after rains they will be out hunting; otherwise, look under rotting wood or loose stones. Spotted newts live in the shallow, weedy waters of lakes or ponds. When floating quietly, they are hard to find, but they are air breathers and can be seen when they swim to the surface, get a gulp of air, then sink down again. Look also for the egg mass in early summer. A ball of clear "jelly" contains the polka dots of the eggs and is fastened to vegetation several inches under the water.

Dace and mussels. Freshwater mussels appear to be immobile creatures, but they can become travelers at an early age. The youngest mussels hitchhike around on the fins of fishes such as dace. Just after hatching from eggs, the tiny mussels have sharp little "teeth" along the edges of their shells and a ticklish urge to snap when the water around them is disturbed. If the disturbance is a swimming fish, the little mussels "taste" its presence and clamp vigorously until they grab a fin. There they live as parasites for several weeks, embedded in the tissue and getting a free ride. Since small fish tend to push their way upstream, when the mussel babies hop off, they are likely to be at a site upstream from their starting point.

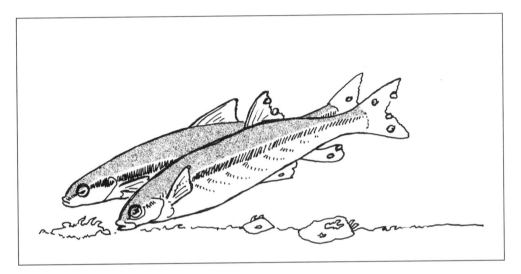

HOW TO FIND HITCHHIKING MUSSELS

This hitchhiking stage tends to occur during the fall and early winter. Catch fish during that time and check for evidence of the little mussels. They would look like small lumps embedded in the fins or the body area near the fins.

Bladderwort and pond plankton. A plant that eats animals is an intriguing notion. A number of unrelated carnivorous plants are able to obtain mineral nutrients in habitats where decaying material is hard to come by. Where the soils are wet, the process of decomposition is limited by a lack of oxygen; therefore, bogs and wetlands are often sites for finding specifically adapted carnivorous plants. The pond weed bladderwort has modified leaves that capture and digest tiny pond creatures. Each bladder is a bubble of tissue with a door and several bristles that act as triggers. A bladder trap is "set" when it is emptied of water, a process that both compresses the sides and seals the door closed. The movement of a passing microscopic creature trips a bristle, the door flies open, and the suction of water draws the animal into the bladder. The door shuts and the digestion begins.

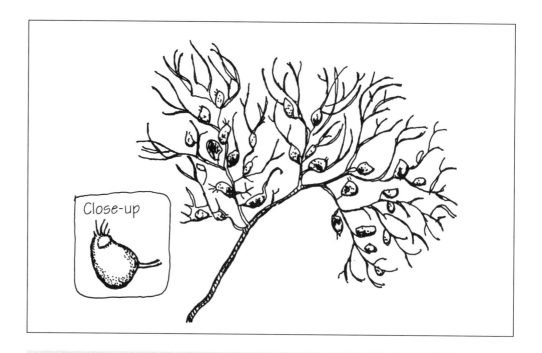

Close-up

HOW TO FIND BLADDERWORT

Bladderwort is a common pond weed of shallow waters, often growing among water lilies and other rooted water plants. You are likely to pull it up by dipping with a net or even a stick. Bladderworts have distinctive lumps, the bladders, scattered throughout their leaf clusters. Dark bladders are filled with food; clear bladders are newly formed. In late summer the bladderworts bloom, sending up a thin stem and a single blossom resembling a small snapdragon. A bladderwort is an indicator of water rich in nutrients and a large plankton population of microscopic animals and larval insects.

Observing Water Flow

To understand how water flow creates a streambed or riverbed, use any opportunity to watch the way water moves. Study the trickling of rainwater down a dirt drive or erosion on a slope. Watch the way the last lines of water move out of a bathtub. Pay attention to how raindrops move off the windshield. The curving strands of water trickling from a cookie sheet you're rinsing in the sink is similar to the huge currents that form the deep bed of the Mississippi River and to the momentary braid of rivulets on a sandy beach when a wave recedes.

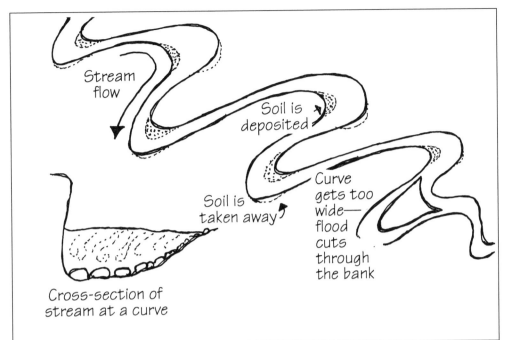

Stream flow

Soil is deposited

Soil is taken away

Curve gets too wide—flood cuts through the bank

Cross-section of stream at a curve

Where flowing water makes a curve, look for a steep bank on the outside of the curve where the faster water flow is taking away soil and a shallow bank on the inside of the curve where slower flow is depositing material.

1 Making a Model Streambed

Materials:

- Sand
- Water from a hose, watering can, or other device that will create a steady flow
- A flat, water-resistant surface that can be raised to make a slope (board, tray, etc.)

Background: Water never moves straight down a slope. Any stream of water functions as ropey strands of water particles moving at slightly different speeds, constantly altered by variation in the land. When the stream meets resistant material, the flow is deflected from its downhill movement and begins to curve away. The outside edge of the water strand picks up speed and force but is restrained into an arc by the slower water in the inner curve. A curving stream tends to move like a pendulum—a swing in one direction results in another swing to the other side. In water, there is the added action of twisting as the liquid strand moves down the streambed.

Procedure: The ways rivers sculpt the land through which they pass is very similar to the ways a trickle of water makes little gullies in a sandy slope. By making your own small model, you can study the larger process and become familiar with the interplay of land and flowing water.

The land for your model could be a wide board (or the back side of a tray or cookie sheet) covered with at least an inch of sand; your stream could be a water hose with some way to vary the force of the flow, such as clamp, a nozzle, or a spigot. To experiment with different conditions, you might collect some rocks, sticks, or leaves to put on or in the sand. Stones or bricks put under one side of the board would change the slope for different effects.

If you want to make a model for long-term or indoor study, you will need both a way to recapture the runoff and sides to retain the sand. One possibility is to line a shallow cardboard box with plastic, creating a gutterlike trough at the bottom to catch and funnel the runoff into a container. The "stream" is siphoned from the container of water in the upper corner; a clamp holds the tube in place to keep the flow constant while other changes are made.

Using your model, try to simulate the following situations and answer the following questions:

1. What is the difference in the flow pattern between land with a small amount of slope and land with a steep slope? (Try to keep the amount of water flow the same so that your only variable is the steepness of slope.)

2. When the flow of water meets an obstacle such as a rock, what is the reaction in terms of the shape of the stream and the effect on the sand?

_____

_____

3. Compare the size of the particles of sand in the runoff with those left in the stream bed. What differences do you notice?

_____

_____

4. Let the water flow from one spot for a while and watch just one curve develop and change. Repeat your procedure and describe the general dynamics of flowing water and the production of curves.

_____

_____

5. To simulate fibers of leaves and rootlets that would be found in the soils where plants grow, mix into the sand some bits of leaves, paper, or pieces of dry spaghetti. What is their effect on the stream flow?

_____

_____

2 Discovering How Water Carves Out Habitats

Materials:

- Quart container
- Serving spoon
- Spoon-sized amounts of flour, fine sand, coarse sand, pea-sized gravel, marble-sized rocks, or similar materials
- Water to fill the container

Background: A stream bed is constantly changing. As the water flows and curves, the more rapidly moving water on the outer edge carves soil from the bank. Where the water flows over roots or rocks, its plunging action creates a pool. The slower water on the inside of a curve drops material, creating sandbars and new land. Animals that live up and down the stream cope with this constant change. Many of the plants and creatures have adaptations that help them make the most of one particular set of conditions within the waterway. As you explore a stream, look for these variables.

- *Temperature.* Water in a pool has a chance to warm up. Check the temperatures of the water just before and just after it leaves a pond or pool. (A household outdoor thermometer will work; make sure water won't wash off the numbers.) Moving water is slightly less likely to freeze when the air falls below freezing. Check where ice first forms in the stream.

- *Amount of material suspended in water.* Rapidly flowing water can carry more sediment than still water. Sediments give the water abrasive power; flood waters full of rock and soil particles can alter landscapes with bulldozer force. The stream at flood level has the power to create new habitats and rearrange old ones.

Procedure: You can experiment with sediment layering and habitat differences with a jar-sized flood. In a quart-sized clear container, mix together your collection of soil materials of varied sizes. Add water nearly to the top and stir or shake the mixture until all the finer ingredients are suspended. (The water looks muddy.) Watch as the water quiets and the materials settle to the bottom. Which material settles first on the bottom? Do the ingredients arrange themselves in distinct layers? Check an hour later. Check again after a day of not moving the jar.

After doing this experiment, explore a shallow stream, especially on the edges of curves or pools and look for examples of stream-sorted particle deposits. Does the

particle size change at the edge of the water on the inside of a curve? A cross section of a streambed usually shows sorting of groups of soil particles. The rapidly moving water on the outside of a curve scours out small particles, exposing larger and heavier rocks. The bank on the inner curve, where you can probably stand near the water, may consist mostly of small stones and sand forming a shallow sandbar.

Survival in Streams

3 Exploring Brook Habitats

Materials:

- Equipment for scooping or netting aquatic creatures (a clear, plastic jar and a small aquarium net will get you started). DO NOT USE GLASS CONTAINERS NEAR A BROOK. THEY WILL BREAK IF YOU DROP THEM.

Background: A brook is full of habitats. Each is defined by the flow of water, oxygen, and nutrients. Every time the stream falls over a rock or gurgles around a log, oxygen-filled air bubbles are blended into the water. As the water flows into the stiller water of a pool, the oxygen is used by the decay organisms that live on the bits of dead plants and animals. During the decay process, nutrients are released into the water. Delicate tubifex worms, adapted to life in low-oxygen water, benefit from the rich nutrient solution of warm backwater pools. When the water eventually flushes over the next little waterfall or cluster of boulders, the oxygen is replenished and the cycle is renewed. Where the water ripples and swirls, larval insects, such as blackflies, hold on to rocks by glueing or clinging and reap a harvest of both nutrients and oxygen.

Procedure: Explore the various habitats of a stream and the creatures who live there. As you examine each find, look for adaptations and behavior that relate to the organism's habitat. For instance, some species of caddis fly glue their silk and stone tubes onto rocks where the flow is strong. Other species are free to move around in the calmer margins of the stream, feeding on a variety of materials they find there.

4 Streamlining: An Adaptation for Survival

Materials:

- Collecting equipment (see previous activity)
- Illustrated identification books on aquatic organisms

Background: You can pick up any stone and tell whether its history included a time spent in moving water. The grinding action of waves or flowing water smooths the edges and rounds the shapes of even hard minerals. Many of the animals that live in streams show a similar sleekness of shape—not because they've been smoothed by moving water, but because any individual born with water-catching projections would be swept downstream, leaving only the streamlined members of the population to breed and produce offspring.

Procedure: Look for examples of streamlined living things both in a stream and in illustrations in guide books to brook life. Make an illustrated list of the shapes of creatures you might find in a stream. Look on the underside of underwater stones. Note the streamlined features of the silk and sand houses made by caddis fly larva and worms.

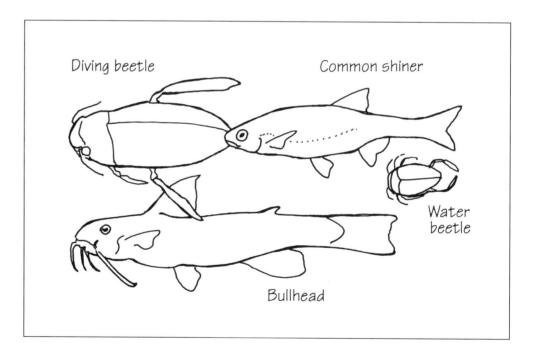

5 Discovering How Streamlining Works

Materials:

- Flowing water from a faucet in a bath or sink or from a hose

Background and Procedure: You can do this simple experiment yourself with streamlined shapes when you are starting a bath. Hold your hands in various positions and observe which shapes cause the most splattering of water. Splattering shows where the water is pushing on your hand; the water that flows around your hand has much less push-power. In terms of survival in a stream, the less an animal is pushed by the water, the less energy it must spend to hold its position. Those creatures that have evolved streamlined shapes to their bodies or the structures they build have more energy available for growth and reproduction than those that must fight against the flow.

The Balance of Life in a Stream

6 How Topsoil Loss Affects Our Fields and Forests

Materials:

- Hammer and nail
- Coffee can
- Cookie sheet
- Soil to fill cookie sheet
- Small pebbles (about 1 cup)
- Small lump of modeling clay
- Several wide-leaved real or plastic plants
- Pitcher of water

Background: The loss of topsoil affects us directly. Nutrient loss in the soil affects the growth and value of plant products. Thousands of tons of valuable nutrients are lost yearly from farmland and forests. The value is easily measured in the tons of fertilizers that must be bought to replace the lost nutrients. People in the agriculture industry are beginning to understand and initiate practices that save the soil, such as reduced plowing, growing cover crops during the winter months, and harvesting select trees instead of clear-cutting.

Procedure: To observe the impact of topsoil loss on agriculture and forestry, prepare a simulated field habitat. Carefully punch many small holes in the bottom of the coffee can with the hammer and nail. Put a layer of pebbles in the bottom of the cookie

Muddy water in a stream or river after a rain means topsoil erosion somewhere upstream.

sheet and cover them with a layer of soil. Place the cookie sheet outdoors on a sheet of newspaper so that the cookie sheet is slightly tilted.

Holding the coffee can over the cookie sheet, pour water into the can, allowing it to "rain" upon your simulated slope. What happens to the slope? What is left if you continue to pour water on the soil?

Set up the slope again, but this time, before you add soil to the cookie sheet, plant several small plants among the pebbles by sticking them into lumps of clay. Fill the tray with soil and provide a rainstorm again. Is there less topsoil erosion when plants are on the slope? Would a layer of grass hold more soil in place? What would be the effect of heavy rain on a virgin forest? a clear-cut area?

7 An Overdose of Nutrients: Algae Overgrowth

Materials:

- Two clear containers of equal size (glass jars are okay)
- Water to fill the containers
- Commercial plant fertilizer ("plant food"), either liquid or dry
- About a spoonful of algae (the slimy green plant found in ponds, streams, and ditches; any water plant with leaves or stems is *not* algae).

Background: In other agricultural situations, too many nutrients in the runoff poisons the water. Where farm animals are penned and their manures accumulate, rainwater washes the water-soluble nutrients such as nitrates and phosphates into nearby ponds and streams in such great quantity that the systems become unbalanced. The most visible result is the overgrowth of algae, but another result is the growth of disease-producing bacteria.

Procedure: Find out how dissolved nutrients affect the growth of water plants in a windowsill experiment. Fill two equal-sized clear glass containers with the same amounts of water. Enrich the nutrient content of one sample by adding two teaspoons of liquid or dry plant food (fertilizer) to the water. Label the enriched sample with the date. (Tape a label on it or write on a piece of masking tape and attach.) Your experimental subject will be algae, the stemless, leafless, green plant found in ditches, ponds, and sunny streams. Put equal measures (one teaspoon or perhaps a few grams) of algae in each container. Start with small amounts so you can get a good idea of any differences in their growth. Place both containers in a sunny window and observe the algae's growth over a week's time. (You may need to replace evaporated water.)

What effect, if any, is the extra nutrient on the algae's growth? Do you notice any other differences, such as smell, color, or rate of evaporation? What do you notice after another week of growth? (In a nutrient-overdosed pond, the decomposition of dead algae can use up all the available dissolved oxygen, resulting in the death of fish and other gill-breathers.)

Some experiments are being done to use the nutrient-rich water to grow water plants commercially and use them as fertilizer. As an added benefit, these plants cleanse the water of other poisons used in agriculture. Collected and processed manures produce methane gas, which could be collected and used to run farming equipment. This recycling of waste holds possibilities for making farming a self-sufficient system.

Dams and Ladders

It used to be that in the spring of every year ocean-living fish would swim up our coastal rivers and streams as far as they could go in order to spawn and lay their eggs. Over the past century we've placed so many obstacles in their paths that the phenomenon is mostly impossible. From colonial water-powered mills that relied upon the damming of brooks to the giant hydroelectric dams and artificial recreational lakes of this century, human activities have blocked the migrations of spawning fish. We also added pollutants to the water that altered its taste. Adult fish,

The series of smaller waterfalls to the side of the big spillway gives spawning fish such as shad a chance to get to the upper reaches of the river where the eggs will be laid.

searching for the streams in which they were spawned, use their sense of taste to test the waters and become confused by the new tastes—enough to change their breeding patterns. Ocean fish are now being successfully reintroduced into our large rivers. Control of pollution and the addition of fish ladders around the larger dams are bringing salmon and shad back to the upper reaches.

How Water Systems Are Cleaned

Marshes are the vast filtering organs of the circulatory system that is a river, working to break down the loads of organic chemicals and filter out the toxins. The deep, spongy soils catch and hold the extra nutrients, supporting dense growths of plants. The marshes are also the nursery areas of many fishes and waterfowl that continue to recycle the nutrients by using them for growth. Water below the marshes is cleaner and more life-supporting than upstream water. Along seacoasts the marshes that form where the river meets the sea are the nursery habitats for the young of many saltwater animals.

When people go about setting up systems for cleaning water for human use, the process approximates that of the river system. The first step is to filter out the loose stuff with sieves and/or with settling tanks.

A second step processes the organic material, those particles and chemicals that can be broken down by helpful bacteria and algae. Aeration, through either waterfalls or fountains, adds oxygen and helps microorganisms grow. Sometimes artificial marshes are created: Water is trickled over mats of slime, which consumes and filters out the pollutants. If the upstream pollution has been too toxic for these methods to succeed, chemicals that break down the poisonously complex molecules are added at a third stage of treatment. Cleaning up our water can be extremely expensive. Upstream control of erosion and pollution is much cheaper.

You can help control downstream pollution by watching what is thrown into your trash. Never dispose of pesticides, herbicides, cleaning fluids, motor oil, batteries, or oil-based paints in regular trash (which might be dumped in the ocean or leak out of a landfill). All of these materials must be placed in steel drums and stored in a special landfill. An even better solution is to avoid buying them altogether. Investigate alternatives; humans didn't always need toxic materials to have fun or live well. (The EPA's *Citizen's Guide to Ground-Water Protection* has excellent information on contaminants to water supplies. Write to the U.S. Environmental Protection Agency, Office of Water, 401 M Street, S.W., Washington, D.C. 20460. A local environmental organization will probably have specific listings for you. If not, write to Massachusetts Audubon Society at South Great Road, Lincoln, MA 01773.

PONDS—QUIET WATER

Characteristics of the Area

Your still-water study site could be a dug pond near a spring or a duck pond in a park. It could be a dammed lake or natural backwater along the course of a watershed. It could be a temporary pond that exists only during the rainy season. When water is held back from flowing, its character changes. As quiet water, it is likely to be a breeding place for fish, insects, and amphibians, where herons, ducks, mink, or raccoons come to hunt. In the quiet water, plants may grow on the water's edge or partially submerged along the banks. Where water slows, silt is deposited, creating a rich nutrient base for vegetative growth and microscopic animals. Soil and vegetation will gradually fill in at the edge of a pond, creating habitat zones of varying degrees of warmth, sunlight, and available oxygen.

Still-water shallows are usually full of life. The nutrient-rich stable environment supports large numbers and varieties of creatures. As you learn to explore the pond by quietly watching or by carefully scooping, you may find that the process of discovering new creatures is satisfying and somewhat addictive. The linked strands

of ecologicial relationships are easy to detect as well. Many different predators, hosts of varied prey, and plants with fascinating adaptations are readily found.

Common Inhabitants

See page 37.

Studying the Area

You will need some sort of net to scoop up pond inhabitants and a light-colored bucket or pan to hold them for observation. A small aquarium net is adequate for shallow dipping, or a sturdy net with a fine mesh, such as those sold with swimming pool supplies, can help you reach farther out or catch larger animals. Frogs, fish, and turtles should not be detained for more than a few minutes. These larger animals have fewer successful offspring, and the adults serve important roles as breeders. The smaller and more abundant animals go right back to doing whatever they were up to when caught and can be observed for a day or so if carefully handled. They can be captured with a sieve, a homemade net of stocking material, or an inexpensive goldfish net.

When you first approach your study area, do so quietly and stealthily. Other hunters may be there: Herons, kingfishers, water snakes, or mink might be hunting the shores. The types of hunters you find will depend on the area in which you live. Frogs and turtles basking in the sun will be frightened into the water by any sudden movements. Fish can see you if you stand close to the edge of the water. First, sit still

for as long as you can and watch; you might see creatures that you would never see if you disrupted the water with a net. As you begin to use your net to scoop material out of the pond, pay attention to what parts of the shoreline are richest in quantity and variety of living things. Are certain animals found only in certain sections? Why do you think that happens? When you bring a net full of plants or mud onto the bank, be careful to return to the pond any material you don't put in your study pan. Mud and plant material are full of microscopic organisms that will die if left on land. Handle every creature gently and as little as possible (many can bite!). Return them to their pond when you are done.

Come back to observe your pond at different times of the year. There will be dramatic changes as the amphibians and insects return to the pond to breed, as their young proceed through their stages of development, and as various populations of predators come to stalk them. Even freezing temperatures do not completely shut down the pond ecosystem; turtles, fish, and even frogs can be active under the ice, and certain creatures, such as fairy shrimp, are more likely to be found during the winter.

Still-water habitats change over the years, becoming shallower, warmer, and more crowded with plants, in a natural progression of silting-in and becoming land. A dramatic drop in a population of plants or animals that had been stable may mean something else, however. All aquatic life forms are very sensitive to pollution; and many poisonous chemicals we use in daily life may enter a pond by rainwater runoff or purposeful dumping (wetlands are still seen as wastelands by many people). Your knowledge and records of such changes could help stop further pollution.

8 Taking a Pond Life Survey

Materials:

- A copy of this activity and/or an illustrated guide to pond life
- Paper, pencil, and a firm surface for drawing
- Collecting equipment (optional)

Background and Procedure: You will learn the most about life in a pond by discovering the names and behaviors of the inhabitants. Some you will see if you sit quietly and observe a portion of the pond edge and shallow water. At first the water will seem empty, but you will soon begin to pick out the small movements and shapes of the inhabitants. If you have a scoop and a container, gently capture specimens for closer looks. Use your paper to make sketches and write down any behaviors that you think help the animal survive in (or on) the water. Find your creature in a pond book and write down any other interesting information you read about.

The following examples are commonly found in still water. Try to find, observe, and record these or similar creatures that you find.

- *Water striders* are just the right weight for water-walking. Tufts of hairs on their feet keep their legs from sticking through the surface film, just as snowshoes keep winter hikers up on the top of the crust of deep snow. Where the striders' feet touch the surface, the water dimples down slightly. Striders are predators. If a small insect drops onto the surface, a strider will zero in on it, guided by the ripples made by the struggling bug. (Offer them the next mosquito you swat.)

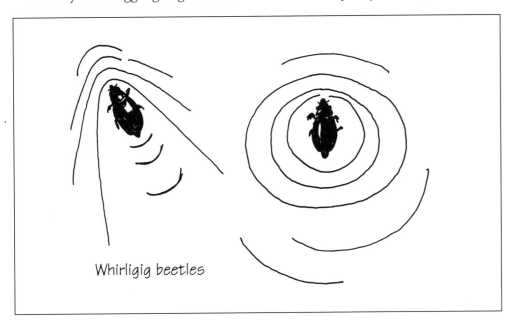

Whirligig beetles

- *Whirligig beetles* sometimes collect on the water's surface in a busy congregation of doodling bodies. Try to follow just one individual—it's almost impossible! The eyes of a whirligig have double vision: a top half to observe what's above and an underwater half for watching under the surface. When threatened from above, a whirligig will dive under the water.

- Both *frogs and turtles* have eyes, ears, and nostrils located close together at the top of their heads. They can float so that most of their body is under the surface, but they can still watch, listen, and breathe. Most frogs come out of the water to hunt

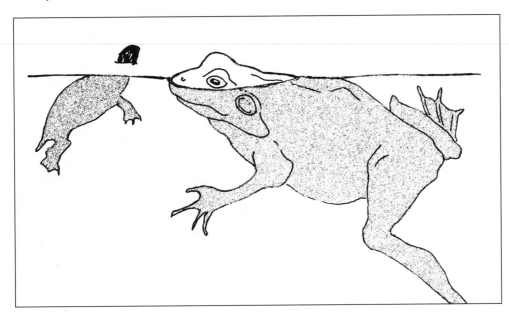

for food and warm up in the sun. Turtles come out only to bask and warm themselves. They hunt in water, and many species must be underwater to swallow effectively. Be careful as you observe them; both turtles and frogs will struggle to get free and will drop from any height as fearlessly as though they were over water; both animals would be injured by a hard landing.

The Water's Surface

A floating leaf can become a "life preserver" for a land insect that has had the misfortune to fall on the pond. To a small insect, the surface of the water has almost an adhesive quality; a moth would not be able to pull its wings free from the grip of the top layer without something like a solid pond leaf on which to grab hold.

Water as a fluid has a tendency to adhere to and attract other water molecules. To observe this, sprinkle several water drops onto a piece of wax paper. Nudge one drop next to another and they will immediately cohere into a single drop.

Surface water is pulled down by the drops below it, forming a denser layer. You can see this surface layer working if you fill up a glass or bottle carefully to the top with cold water, then add just a few more drops. If you look across the top, you can see that the water has risen *above* the rim but is held in the glass by the surface film.

A waxy coating on the leaves of the water lily keeps water from collecting on the surface where it might block sunlight or cause the leaf to rot. Stiff, spongy veins float and support the leaf-like struts in an umbrella, and rubbery, flexible stems hold leaves against the pull of the current or a sudden rise in water level. The plants also serve as walking surfaces for hunting spiders, small frogs, and turtles. Look on the underside of leaves for clusters of eggs, tubes made by worms or caddis fly larvae, and soft sponges.

9 Experimenting with Surface Tension

Materials:

- A sewing needle
- A bowl (at least as wide as the width of your hand)
- Water to fill the bowl
- Small amounts of liquid soap, salt, oil, hot water

Background and Procedure: Experiment with how the surface film tension is affected by a variety of water conditions. Your indicator will be a floating sewing needle. Fill your bowl with cool water and practice dropping the needle so that it floats on the surface. (What happens if you let the needle drop point first?); several same-sized bowls will enable you to do your experiment more quickly.

Once you have the needle floating on the water add substances to the water to see how the surface tension is affected, that is, if the needle will sink. Try a drop of detergent, some salt, a drop of oil, or hot water instead of cold. (Don't drop the additives right onto the needle.) Experiment with each substance a number of times to make sure that it is the additive that makes the difference. Experiment with combinations of conditions to see if some lessen the effects of others. For instance, can oil on a needle make it less likely to sink when detergent is added? (Do any aquatic animals use oil to increase their buoyancy?) After studying the ways striders stay on the surface, can you come up with modifications that would keep your "needle-bug" afloat in hot water?

Making Waves: Water Insect "Sonar"

In addition to being able to locate prey by responding quickly to ripples on the surface film, water striders can also send ripple messages by vibrating their legs. A male strider that has found a bit of soft vegetation for an egg-laying site will broadcast his find across the water. An interested female will respond with a slightly different vibration. If another male intrudes, he will be confronted by an aggression message from the defending male. This special kind of "sonar," the sending and reading of vibrations on the surface layer, allows many of the surface insects to communicate as well as maneuver. A whirligig beetle also can sense the location of other objects, including the courses of other whirligigs, by responding to the waves returning from its own wake.

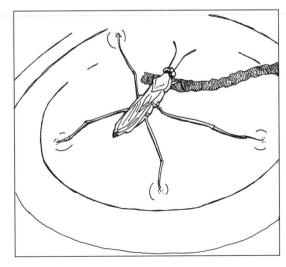

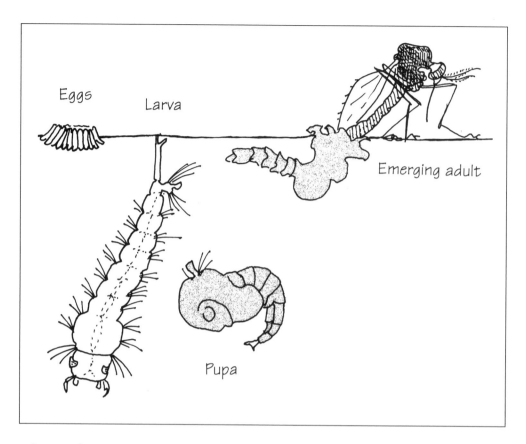

The Mighty Mosquito and the Problem of Surface Tension

An animal as small as a mosquito must deal with the water's surface throughout its life stages. As an air-breathing larva, it must have a breathing tube capable of puncturing the surface layer each time it rises to breathe. In the pupal stage, it must rest near the surface most of the time, breathing through an opening surrounded by special hairs that push through the surface film. The day it hatches into a winged adult must be windless and the surface calm. Were the mosquito to tilt over and touch the water as it climbed up out of its pupal case, it would be trapped by the film. Returning to lay eggs, the female mosquito must deal with the dangerous film again as she carefully lays a raft of eggs while balancing near the surface.

10 Clustered Interaction on the Water

Materials:

- Note-taking or drawing equipment

Background and Procedure: Although some water striders seem to jump on each other occasionally (by mistake or as aggression?), whirligigs often gather in a spinning group, yet never seem to get in each other's way. This clustered interaction is not unusual among pond inhabitants.

When you see pond insects involved in clustered interaction, keep track of the times and the behaviors you observe. What function might the gatherings serve for the population of creatures? Is the gathering a response to localized food? Is the site warmer or more open or protected? Would you characterize the interactions as aggressive, with some individuals trying to drive off others? Do you observe mating (a smaller male staying on the back of a larger female for several minutes)? Look for egg-laying; the female would be depositing eggs in floating vegetation or below the surface. Try to imagine some other possible interpretations of insect swarming; much of insect behavior has yet to be deciphered.

Breathing Under Water

All animals need oxygen in their bloodstreams to stay alive. Aquatic animals are either air breathers or water breathers. The air breathers take oxygen out of the air, either directly, at the surface, or from a SCUBA tank, a bubble they take down with them. The water breathers are able to absorb oxygen dissolved in the water through thin-skinned and blood-filled gills, a process that does not function in air. Many pond organisms, such as frogs and dragonflies, start out as water breathers and mature into air breathers. Some wintering animals, with their metabolisms greatly slowed, are able to absorb all the oxygen they need through their skin. Chilled and inactive turtles can breathe through the skin in their cloaca, an enlarged section of their anal opening.

11 Solutions for Getting a Breath Under Water

Materials:

- Guide book on pond life

Background and Procedure: Use guide books to look up the natural history of some of the animals you find in the pond to find out how each solves the problem of gas exchange. (Every creature that breathes in oxygen must also get rid of its waste, carbon dioxide.) Every vertebrate will have its air exchange system up front (nostrils, gills), and every insect will have gills or tubes along the sides of its abdomen, where the breathing spiracles are located. Here is a partial list of pond animals and their various ways of breathing.

- *Backswimmer:* While the backswimmer floats at the surface, special hair tufts break through the surface film, letting air move into the air pockets created by hairs on its the belly (the side facing the surface).

- *Mosquito:* The larva breathes air at the surface through pipes in its tail section. The large-headed pupa has breathing apparatus located at the back of its head.

- *Water Scorpion:* A snorkle at the end of its abdomen lets the predacious bug hunt while drifting at the surface, head downward.

- *Dragonfly nymph:* Water is drawn into a large vent at the end of the abdomen. Gill-like structures inside extract oxygen at every intake. The nymph is able to use its expulsion power to "jet" through the water to escape danger.

- *Damselfly nymph:* Three feather-shaped gills float from the end of the abdomen.

- *Mayfly nymph:* Furry-looking gills are clustered along the sides of the abdomen.

- *Salamander larvae:* Densely branching gills stick out on the sides of the newly hatched larvae. Salamanders that leave the water gradually develop inner lungs and become air breathers, even if they return to live in the pond.

- *Frog and toad tadpoles:* Diminutive gills may be visible in just-hatched larvae, but the gills later become covered by a fold of skin, giving the tadpoles a shape like a comma. The development of lungs precedes the growth of legs, causing older tadpoles to become air gulpers at the surface.

- *Fish:* The bright red gills of fish are located on either side of the fish's head, under protective gill covers. The covers act as a bellows, pulling water through the mouth, over the gills, and then out the gill opening.

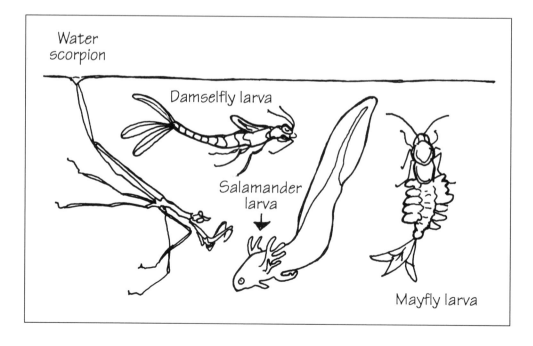

Feeding in and around Ponds

12 Adaptations of Predators

Materials:

- Paper
- Pencil, crayons, or markers

Background and Procedure: If you were assigned the task of designing a predator to live in a pond, what adaptations would you design? Consider first your problem: Water is a dense medium and is hard to move through quickly enough to catch a swimming prey, that if caught, must be held tightly and killed quickly to avoid injury to the predator. Consider some land-living predators, including small ones such as praying mantis and tiger beetles, and think about whether their predatory behaviors and adaptations could be modified for the underwater world. Make up several aquatic predators. Start with a familiar land predator and modify it to live in an aquatic environment. (This activity is fun when several people work together on one animal.)

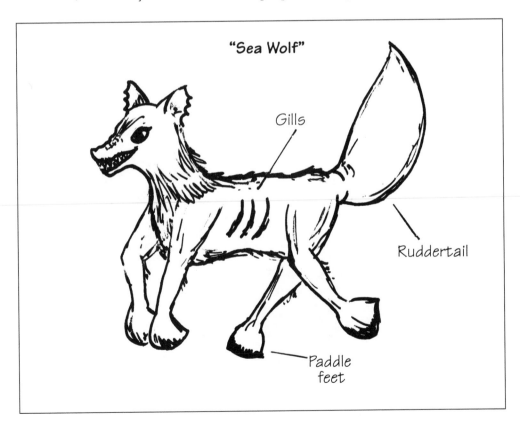

"Sea Wolf"

Gills

Ruddertail

Paddle feet

After you have designed your own predators, look carefully at the adaptations of actual pond predators. Find some living examples if possible, and use field guides to learn about their behaviors. Some common pond predators are water scorpions, giant water bugs, backswimmers, predacious diving beetles, dragonfly larvae, and snapping turtles.

13 Dragonflies: The Falcons of the Pond

Materials:

- Notebook or paper and cardboard support
- Pen or pencil

Background: Move slowly up to a dragonfly as it sits on its perch and look at all the features that make it a superb predator. Its body is streamlined; large clusters of muscles in the thorax (chest area) drive its strong but lightweight wings. When moving to capture prey, the long back legs trail down to form a stiff scoop. Almost all of its head consists of two eye globes, each one made up of hundreds of individual "eye-pieces." Each eye facet transmits the image of its entire environment, seen from a slightly different view. Since it can see all around, any movement catches its attention. You can watch the dragonfly shifting its head and scanning every passing object—even planes! Note which kinds of movements trigger it to fly out and investigate.

A perching dragonfly (or damselfly) is probably overlooking an area it knows

Damselflies mating. The female reaches into a pocket in the male's chest where he previously deposited his sperm packet.

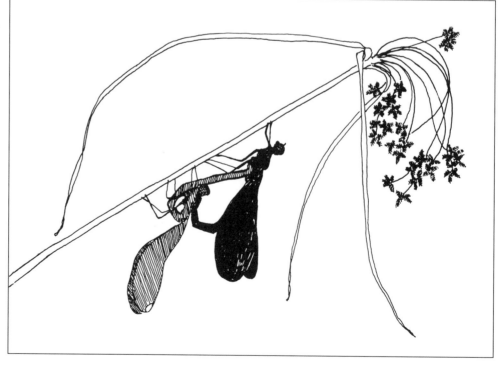

well and even claims as a territory. Territorial behavior includes chasing other dragon-flies of the same species or returning to the same perch after a chase or to eat its catch. By keeping the area clear of other males, the dragonfly is able to claim any females that move through its flight zone. A female that is interested in mating hovers or alights, allowing the male to attach the end of his abdomen behind her head. Locked in this position, she is able to reach with her abdomen into a special cavity in his chest to get the packet of sperm he has previously placed there. Often the pair stay joined while the female deposits her newly fertilized eggs beneath the pond surface. Perhaps his weight helps her break through the surface film; certainly his position keeps other males from mating with the female and supplanting his genetic contribution.

Procedure: To get an idea of how a dragonfly spends its time, spend some of your time watching one. Observe just one individual for at least fifteen minutes. Repeat the observation time at intervals. Record how long it spends in various activities. Possible behaviors would include perching, flying to hunt or drive off other dragonflies, courtship, and mating. Add other behaviors if you can. Working with another person might help with the problem of watching both the insect and your watch. The drag-onflies' interactions of aggression or mating are fairly easy to interpret and define. Other behaviors, such as the dense congregations that swarm over fields on summer afternoons, are not well understood. Your observations and interpretations may add to our understanding of these complex creatures.

Optical Illusions: Problems of Spear-Fishing Predators

Because of the attraction of a large quantity of organisms living in pond water, a great variety of predators can be found near still-water habitats. None of the predacious birds have problems getting below the pond surface, but the water presents them with another difficulty—defraction: the bending of light rays as they pass through water. When you are watching a tadpole swimming along, it is not really where it appears to be. The image of the tadpole is refracted as it passes from the water into the air. You can probably tell where the tadpole is well enough to net it, but if you were a heron or a kingfisher, with only big, sharp tweezers as a catching tool, you would miss your supper if you grabbed at the image you saw instead of compensating for the refraction and stabbing at the space just below the image.

This seemingly bent stick illustrates the defraction illusion that could cause an inexperienced heron to miss its fish

14 Looking for Signs of Feeding at the Edge of the Pond

Materials:

- Notebook or paper and clipboard
- Pen or pencil

Background: The lives of many animals overlap at the edge of the pond. Warblers fly down from the treetops to drink, deer come out of the woods for water, and deep-water fish breed in the shallows. The abundance of sunlight, water, warmth, and nutrients produces quantities of succulent plants as well as succulent plant-eaters; predators cruise through at all times of day. Although you might miss seeing the following animals, look for their signs along the water's edge.

Procedure: Be a pond life detective. Take a notebook or clipboard and paper and go around the edge of the pond. Record and describe every evidence of feeding you find. Look for any of the following:

- *A narrow path of trampled vegetation leading from the water; perhaps some nibbled stubs.* Muskrats often pull out of the water at the same place on their daily searches for land plants to eat. They may drop a mussel in such a place, returning for it after it has died so that the task of prying it open is easier.

- *Scattered remains of small animals, overturned rocks and logs.* Raccoons are excellent shallow-water fishers, using their sensitive fingers to feel for a flicker of leg or fin. Only the inedible parts would be left by these omnivorous eaters. Rocks and small logs are disturbed by raccoons in search of mussels, frogs, crayfish, or salamanders.

- *A partly consumed fish or frog, surrounded by cat-sized paw prints but showing* five *toe pads.* Mink are reckless predators of the water's edge, often attacking animals larger than they can eat at one sitting. Usually, the extra food is either stashed in a burrow or covered with leaves to be eaten later.

- *Toe prints in the mud like a huge hen's foot.* Herons of all sizes will hunt at the smallest ponds for frogs, tadpoles, and fish. During the last weeks of summer, especially, herons wander along water courses searching for untapped food sources. Herons often defecate just as they take flight; look for a large splash of "white wash" near the end of the tracks.

- *Frogs hopping frantically* out *of the water*. Water snakes usually cruise the shallows of a pond, their heads just out of the water, perhaps because a frog is more vulnerable right when it jumps into the water and a snake has a better chance of catching it as it begins to swim. Banded brightly when young, the older, larger water snakes are often almost black. If caught, they will bite, but are not poisonous. CAUTION: IN SOUTHERN AREAS A BLACK SNAKE NEAR THE WATER COULD BE THE POISONOUS WATER MOCCASIN OR COTTONMOUTH.

- *An area on the ground where light surface material is disturbed and fallen leaves are overturned*. Grackles are meticulous hunters, using their bills to turn over every fallen leaf as they stride, hop, and wade along the edge of the pond. Although their nesting trees may not be nearby, they know very well how to harvest the wealth of small creatures found on the edge of the pond.

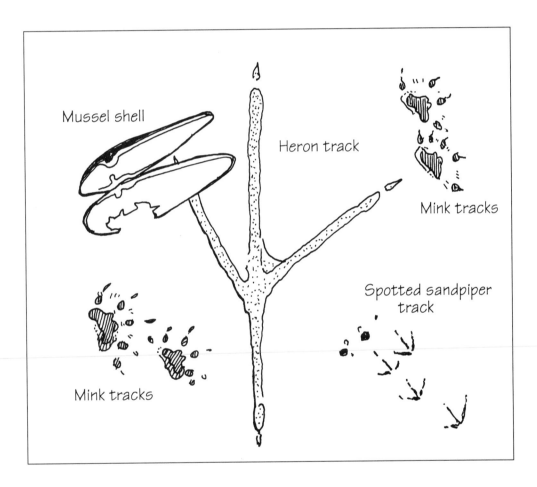

15 Baiting and Marking to Observe Behaviors

Materials:

- Small chunks of meat
- Marking medium (light-colored chalk or correcting fluid)
- Note-taking equipment

Background and Procedure: If you have the opportunity to return to the pond on a regular basis, try doing some baiting to attract some of the scavengers and carnivores of the pond. Attach a small amount (candy-bar-sized) of meat (any kind) to a weight such as a rock (or anchor it with a toothpick) and sink it where it is covered by the water but still visible. A variety of animals such as turtles, tadpoles, and snails will be attracted to the meat, and you will be able to observe their feeding methods.

If snails are common, you might want to try marking the shells of twenty or so individuals so you can keep track of their dispersal patterns when the bait is finished. Make the marks with a water-resistant, but not permanent, medium, such as a white correcting fluid or soft chalk. Put the mark on the topmost part of the shell, away from the lip and the animal's body. Check on the rate of snail dispersal on a daily basis if possible. Are certain areas *not* visited by snails? Do snails show any patterns of movement over the course of the day?

The decaying meat will also feed the bacteria of the pond and cause pollution on a small scale. If your pond is small, an area you can easily wade across, baiting may do damage to the ecosystem by overloading the water with bacteria. You may need to anchor the bait with toothpicks in a strongly flowing stream. Try using only tiny pieces of meat; the "taste" of the decaying meat will travel throughout the water and attract any scavengers that live there. Come back at night with a flashlight to check on nocturnal visitors.

Escaping Predation

16 Making Models of Camouflaged Pond Animals

Materials:

- Paper (newsprint or typing paper)
- Crayons or markers for coloring
- Your field sketches or illustration in a pond study book
- Glue, staples, or tape
- String or coat hangers (for suspending the models)

  Note: Instead of making separate models, this activity could be done as a mural of many drawings.

Background: Hiding in water presents an interesting challenge. Rapid escape in a small pond may be impossible. Many pond creatures opt to hide. For most, a covering that matches their surroundings provides the best chance of survival. But one must be camouflaged from predators who come from above as well as those below. A predator looking down will see a view of mostly browns and greens; a predator looking up will see the light above the surface. Many of the pond creatures that swim or float, including ducks, frogs, fish, and turtles, show a color combination that looks

dark from above and light from below: mottled browns on their backs, whites and greys on their undersides.

Procedure: The subtleties of camouflage coloring can best be appreciated by making your own drawings of pond creatures. Look at colored illustrations, if possible. Make the creature of your choice (fish work well) larger than life, out of a lightweight paper such as contsruction paper or newsprint, then cut out your animal's shape *plus* a duplicate. Use the duplicate to represent the other side of the creature. Color both sides. Staple or glue the shapes together, leaving several inches open so you can stuff the body with tissue or crumpled paper, then tape or staple close the opening. Your creation can be attached to a long stick or coat hanger as a puppet or it might join other paper pond creatures as a wall hanging or mobile. You may wish to create an entire underwater scene, including all the animals you have found in your pond.

17 Pond Swim Meet: Shapes and Devices of Swimmers

Materials:

- Pond animals and water from their pond
- A shallow container (cake or dish pan)
- A ruler
- Pencil and paper
- Stopwatch with second hand

Background: Small aquatic creatures swim about in a pond in a wonderful variety of ways. Some achieve slow locomotion by waving lots of legs; others move by twists and jerks; some paddle or row. The pedestrian-looking dragonfly larva can be moving slowly on legs one minute, then suddenly transform into a jet-powered projectile by pushing water out an opening in its tail.

Procedure: Study and compare the swimming modes of animals you find in your study area. Place them in a wide container in water from the pond. Remove any plant material the animals might hide under. Gently position an animal with a stick or pencil, then time and measure its movements. Make a chart or graph that shows the relative distances, such as the example on the next page:

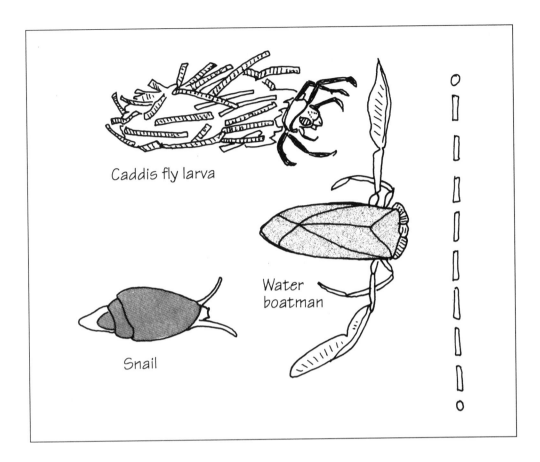

Caddis fly larva

Water boatman

Snail

ANIMAL	DISTANCE TRAVELED IN 15 SECONDS
Water Tiger (*Diving beetle larva*)	I————I
Snail	I-I
Mosquito larva	I———I
Damselfly larva	I—————I
Dragonfly larva (Jetting)	I————————————I

The Foundation of the Pond Food Chain

Land plants have special structures for coping with the drying conditions of life on land. Woody stems hold the leaves up to the light and protect the water supplied by the widespread roots. Both the sunlight and the water are used in the synthesis of sugars, which may then be moved or stored by the plant. Only plants can create sugar energy, and this fabulous knack makes them essential to the growth of every creature of land or water.

18 Pond Plants—Charting their Habitats and Adaptations

Materials:

- Any clothing or equipment to help you explore the pond from the shore out to a safe depth. (Could be as simple as old sneakers or as elaborate as a canoe.)
- Measuring stick or a string with a weight for measuring
- Note-taking material

Background: Pond plants need water and air, just as land plants do; but in the pond, there is lots of water and not much air. Water plants grow in ways that express the different challenge of underwater life. The surface-floating leaves of water lilies have pores for gas exchange located on their upper surfaces, instead of on their undersides like land plants. Water lily roots function as storage areas and anchors, and their stems contain spongy tissues that store air and serve as flexible leashes between roots and leaves. Plants that live completely underwater, such as elodea, are able to recycle their own gases, storing the oxygen produced during daylight hours, then storing carbon dioxide as it is released at night. (Oxygen is recycled during the growth process and carbon dioxide is needed for photosynthesis.)

Procedure: You can best get a feeling for adaptations of water plants by relating the structures of each species to the depth of the water where it lives. Measure and record the depths at which you find particular species of plants. (Use a stick with marked units or a weighted string that can be lowered until the weight rests on the

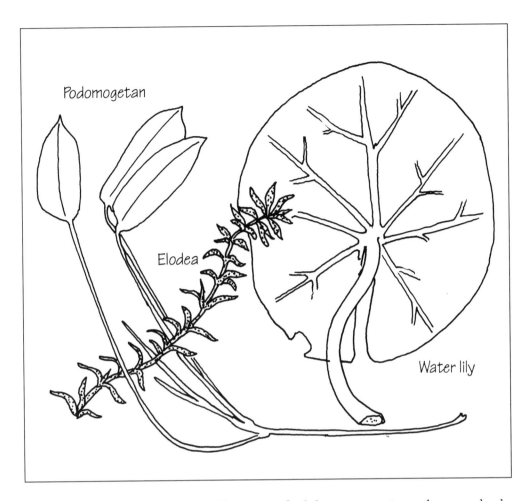

Podomogetan

Elodea

Water lily

bottom, then raised and measured.) Can you find the same species at the same depth elsewhere in the pond? As you wade or paddle away from the edge of the pond's bank, investigate the adaptations of the different plants you find. Return the plants to their correct habitat. Look for the following attributes:

- Waxiness of the leaf to help keep the leaves above the surface
- Strengthening structures keep the leaves or stems upright or outstretched
- Spongy tissues keep the leaves afloat or for possible use as air storage
- Thickening or dense tissue in perennial roots where starch could be stored for next season's growth
- Stems or roots that help a plant spread thoughout a habitat by vegetative repro-
  duction.

Do you think any of the plants you find could survive if the pond dried up?

19 Aquatic Micro-Monsters

Materials:

- Eyedropper or container for scooping
- Light-colored shallow pan for observing tiny organisms
- Pond life book
- Hand lens
- Microscope

Background: The tiniest plants and animals of the pond might seem to be the oddest. Books on pond life usually have illustrations of microscopic organisms, but with a microscope you can see for yourself. Hydras, seed shrimp, and daphnia are visible with a hand lens and can be collected by using a jar or a net made of stocking mesh. You'll need a microscope with a magnification of 100X to 800X to see the creatures' features and behaviors. (A 10X hand lens is not powerful enough; it will magnify the object only ten times its size.) Since the shapes and habits of these creatures are so wonderfully odd, it helps to familiarize yourself with their characteristics first by reading about them and looking at pictures. Then, when you get a look at the creatures firsthand, you'll be less likely to overlook something special or important.

Procedure: Since you can't see many of the "animalcules" of the microcosm, you have to explore various microhabitats to find them. Try scraping the surface of an underwater stone and looking at the material under a microscope. Then look at the surface of a decaying leaf or twig from the pond bottom, or search the undersurface of a floating plant. Since many creatures swim about, use a straw to collect at the surface, near the bottom, or in the warm waters near the edge of the bank. Like sea plankton, many pond plankton come to the surface during the dark hours, so you might try collecting at night.

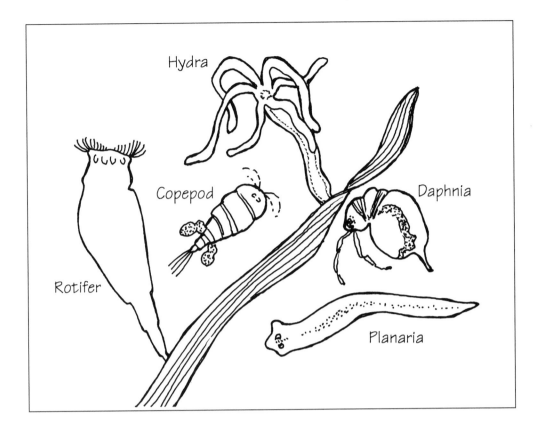

20 Food Chains: The House That Jack Built

Tiny as the microscopic creatures are, without them there would be no life in the pond. The tiny animals feed on the tiny plants, the single-cell algaes. Many of the young of larger animals feed on the tiny animals or else feed on their predators. These microscopic organisms are extremely vulnerable to environmental conditions. Changes in the pond's chemistry, through petrochemical runoff or acid precipitation, quickly poison many species. Even silty conditions, such as the muddy waters created by the bottom-feeding goldfish released by well-intentioned people, can block the sunlight needed by the algae, effectively destroying the whole ecosystem.

Any description of the strands of lives connected by predator/prey relationships resembles the poem, "The House That Jack Built." A pond poem would start with the sunlight that powered the algae that fed the microscopic animals that feed every other animal and so on to a predator such as a sunfish or kingfisher. Devise your own sequenced pond poem, using plants and animals you have observed and read about. Make illustrations of your characters, showing them in the act of capturing some food energy.

The Seasonal Reunion

As is true for most of the earth's ecosystems, the return of longer days of sunlight in spring initiates the beginning of the summer growth cycle. As the water warms, the plants begin to photosynthesize and grow. The increase in plant food triggers an explosion in microscopic animal life and sets the stage for the big spring reunion.

21 Looking for Signs of Breeding

Materials:

- Flashlight

Background: The first warm, rainy nights after the cold weather of winter marks the time of awakening and return for the animals that breed in the pond. Adult creatures that have graduated to land life return to the pond to breed and lay eggs; the underwater adolescents, the nymphs and tadpoles, are still completing their last stages of growth and change preceding adulthood. You might hear the returning frogs before you see them; the male frogs and toads call noisily, and the females are attracted to their voices. Male salamanders, such as the spotted salamander, often move toward the pond on the same nights as the first frogs start calling. They can be seen crossing

Adult spotted salamanders return to the pond in the early spring. Sperm-filled spermatophores are deposited by males. Females are fertilized by gathering the spermatophores; then they lay their eggs on submerged twigs.

roads or gathering in the shallows. Each amphibian species has its breeding time: the smaller frogs first, then the toads, and the larger bullfrogs and green frogs still later.

Procedure: It is definitely worth the effort to make nightly trips of your own to observe the nocturnal goings-on. Predators will be scouting the pond with you. Water snakes, garter snakes, raccoons, foxes, and skunks may be hunting in the shallows. You must have a flashlight, both to locate animals and to keep from stepping on creatures on their way to the water. Hold the light up near your eyes, either beside your head or on top, and scan the borders of the pond. The light will pick up shining eyes of hidden animals. Even the eyes of small spiders at the edge of the pond will be visible as tiny, glowing lights. You are actually seeing your light shining off the reflective surface in back of their eyes. Flashlights that you can strap on your head are available in camping or sports equipment stores.

Try cupping your hands behind your ears to help you find particular singers. By extending and enlarging your sound-capturing ear flaps, you can locate a calling, hidden peeper by moving your head back and forth. Also try hitting rhythmically at the water surface with a long stick. Curious creatures, including predators, may come to investigate.

The Watershed

The streams, ponds, lakes, rivers, and marshes we have been considering are collectively called the watershed, the land-bound portion of a much vaster system that includes clouds and rain, the water cycle.

22 Using Maps to Study Your Watershed

Materials:
- Map of your area (A road map might help, but check your municipal offices or library for maps showing local land and water systems.)

Background: Wherever you live, you live on or near a source of water. Perhaps you live where water collects and begins to flow over the surface; perhaps you live where waters gather in a river or move as seepage underground. Perhaps you live where a river flows into the sea or on a coast where larger waters intermingle with currents carrying material from the inland waters.

Procedure: Use a map and try to follow the whole, treelike system of water movement in your watershed. Talk with other people and use your library to answer the following questions: (1) What happens upstream? (2) How does your town or neighborhood affect the water? (3) What happens to the water downstream? (4) At what point does your water become part of larger ocean currents? (5) Where do they go and what effects do the currents have?

Look around your home area for evidence of how water sources influenced the placement and growth of towns. Your town might have grown up around a harbor or a recreational lake. You might live near farmland that is irrigated by deep wells or water brought from distant mountains. You might notice old mill buildings that once depended on water flow to power their machines.

Using a local map, follow upstream from the area you have been studying. You will eventually come to a place where the water collects and becomes a stream, or emerges from the ground as an underground spring. If the origin of your stream is collected rainwater, from what other area does the rain—that is, the rain clouds—come? Did your rain clouds form over water or over land? Are there smoke-producing industries in the area where the clouds form? Watch local weather reports for clues to where your rainstorms originate.

23 Charting the Effects of Acid Rain

Materials:

- Soil or water testing kit
- Eye-dropper or scoop for taking the sample
- Distilled water for cleaning the sample-taker between samples

Background: The acidification of ponds and lakes has resulted in the death of whole aquatic ecosystems over the past twenty years. The effect was first noticed after the enactment of laws meant to promote environmental health, namely the reduction of ash release from industrial smokestacks. It soon became obvious that the ash had served to neutralize the acid-forming chemicals that were also being sent up with the smoke. Because the manufacturing costs of reducing the acids was seen as prohibitive and because clear proof of which industry was causing the problem was hard to collect, the acidification of rain and particle fallout went uncontrolled. Now we have large lakes with water so acidic that nothing can live in them. The frogs no longer sing, and no fishing is worth the effort, either by humans or herons.

This problem requires enacting laws and fines against industries and being willing to pay our share when the costs of the cleanup are passed on to the consumers.

We can help by reducing our use of gasoline engines and supporting incentives to develop energy industries that do not burn fossil fuels as their initial process.

Procedure: You can keep track of the acidification of local water supplies with soil or water testing kits purchased at garden supply stores or test kits for monitoring blood or urine samples, available from pharmacies. Follow the directions given with the kit, taking special care to use cleaned equipment for each sample gathered. Distilled water for cleaning is often available at grocery stores. If you are careful to use distilled water as your base, you can even get an idea of what changes are occurring by using an acid-indicator such as red-cabbage water. (See method in Activity 23, Measuring Acidity, page 150) Try to measure the water at regular intervals over a year's time. If supplies or time are limited, record the test results over several weeks, especially before and after a rain.

Fields and Borders

PASTURES, PRAIRIES,

EDGES OF PLAYING FIELDS,

AND VACANT LOTS

Woodchuck

Daddy longlegs

Red fox

Song sparrow

Sumac

Daisy fleabane

Brown wasp

Crab-grass

Crab spider

Ambush bug

Black swallowtail

Black-eyed Susan

Goldenrod

E very untended and open piece of land is full of examples of ecological relationships. Plants grow densely in the direct sunlight, attracting a large variety of
plant-eaters and their predators. Plant and animal life cycles tend to be short
and seasonal. The pathways of energy transfer can easily be traced as light energy is
captured by plants, then used for the growth of leaf, flower, fruit, or stem. If the plants
are consumed, the energy is transferred again, into the animal organism. On the surface of the soil, more animals are turning litter into soil nutrients, ready for recycling.
Learning about field ecology helps us understand the systems used to produce food in
the fields we make, for people are the foremost makers of meadows, fields, and pastures. There are few human cultures that do not either use or create open areas to
supply themselves with food. By studying the ecology of fields we can find useful
analogies of how to best use and care for the open areas we depend on for our own
survival. In a way, we are ourselves creatures of the fields and edges. Now we need to
find ways to use that ecosystem without wasting or damaging its productivity.

Characteristics of the Area

A field occurs wherever an open piece of land gets a chance to grow plants for a summer or more. When a lawn or playground goes uncut, a piece of farmland or hayfield
goes unused, or a section of bare soil is allowed to grow freely for a year or so, the
grasses and weedy plants grow up and begin to provide homes, cover, and food for a
large variety of creatures. Your study area may be the undeveloped area near a shopping mall or industrial park, the unmowed edge of a playing field, or a portion of
lawn left to grow for a season. Your town conservation committee may have set aside
farmlands as conservation areas that are kept open by occasional mowings. Concentrate your studies in any of these types of fields.

Common Inhabitants

The following plants and animals are commonly found in most of the field and field edge habitats of North America. If the area you study does not have all of these species, look for similar species and relationships that might be there.

PLANTS	ANIMALS
Woody trees and shrubs	Song sparrow
Sumac	Vole
Juniper (also called red cedar)	Ant
Chokecherry	Lady bug
Poplar	Orb-weaving spider
Shrub Rose	Black swallowtail butterfly
	Ambush bug
Herbaceous plants	Bee fly
Black-eyed Susan	Tent caterpillar
Ox-eye daisy	Harvestman (daddy-longlegs)
Goldenrod	Monarch butterfly
Aster	Milkweed beetle
Milkweed	Sparrow hawk (kestrel)
Various grasses	Red fox
Daisy fleabane	Cottontail rabbit
	Woodchuck
	Coyote

Relationships to Look for

Ambush bugs on goldenrod blossoms. When a goldenrod blossoms, it becomes the feeding platform for many insects. Beetles, bees, wasps, flies, and butterflies all fly in to feed on the nectar and pollen found within the many little flowers. But hiding in the floral clusters, the ambush bug waits to eat. Its food will be the nectar feeders. The mottled coloring of an ambush bug and its irregular body shape blend in with the varied shapes and colors of the goldenrod. The predator moves very little, and the feeding insects are likely to pass closely as they move from flower to flower. When near enough, the bug pounces, grasping the victim tightly in its strong pincer forelegs. The piercing mouth then injects digestive enzymes into the captured insect. Once the inner parts are reduced to a "soup," the liquid material is sucked out.

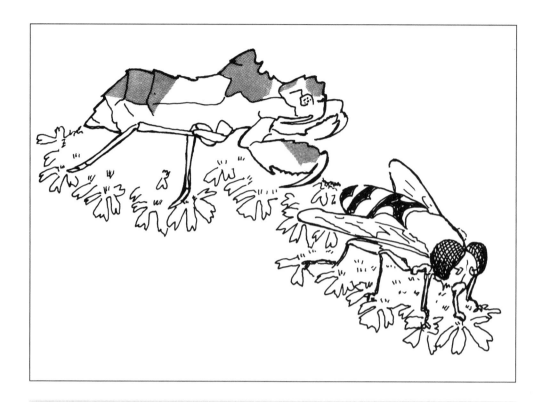

HOW TO FIND AMBUSH BUGS

Although the bugs themselves are hard to spot, if you notice a bee or a butterfly lying on a blossom at an odd angle of repose, it is probably being processed by an ambush bug. Look next to the female for the smaller male ambush bug who may share the female's catch.

Milkweed, monarchs, and milkweed beetles. Fields that are utilized by grazing animals such as cows and horses are likely to have fully grown uneaten milkweed plants among the closely cropped dandelions and grasses. Milkweed sap is extremely bitter to taste, even toxic in large doses. For most insects, even a small dose is too much, but several beetles, bugs, and butterflies have evolved chemical responses that neutralize the toxin. The presence of the chemical in their bodies even gives them some protection, since an animal that eats the beetle or butterfly will get such a bad experience that it will learn to avoid further attempts. Many milkweed insects come in bright colors, often reds, which may help predators identify insects with similar poisons. Similar colorations even give some nontoxic insects false immunity. The adult viceroy butterfly has no toxic aftertaste, but its resemblance to the milkweed-infused monarch butterfly gives it some margin of safety from butterfly-eating birds.

Milkweed beetles are also able to consume milkweed leaves. But a milkweed is not a helpless victim—a leaf is able to sense tissue damage and increase the sap content of toxin and latex, which gums over the wound (and an insect's jaws). The bright red beetles have evolved a strategy for keeping their leaf edible: They bite into a main vein, starting the flow of sap. They then climb up the leaf and eat the now defenseless tissue above the bite.

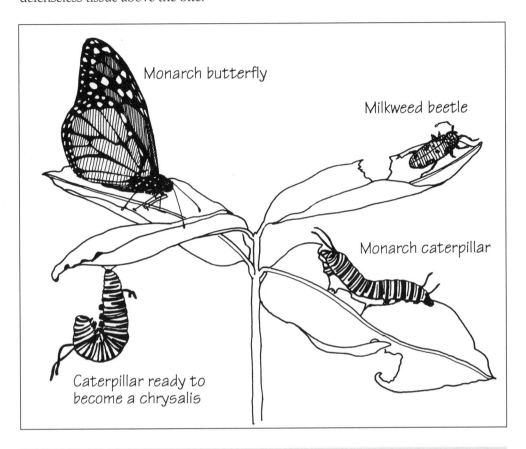

Monarch butterfly

Milkweed beetle

Monarch caterpillar

Caterpillar ready to become a chrysalis

HOW TO FIND MILKWEED

The milkweed plants are usually easy to spot. Each plant is about three feet tall, and their large, oval leaves grow off the single stem in pairs. Where you find one, you'll find several to many; milkweed can colonize an area through radiating underground stems. (The greater the number of plants, the older the colony.) Investigate broken or eaten leaves to find beetles or caterpillars. If you handle the sticky white sap, be very careful not to touch sappy fingers to your eyes, mouth, or nose—the strong alkaloid toxins in the sap can burn tender skin areas.

Orb-weaver spiders and bees. A spider's web, bright with dew, is the classic image of life in a summer meadow. Minus the dew, it is also an extremely efficient, nearly invisible, means of capturing food for the orb-weaver spider. Some species (the *Argiope* are common examples) add broad white zigzags of silk in the center of their webs. The irregular pattern helps hide a spider's shape as she hangs in the center, but the web seems more visible. Some ecologists wondered how the pattern helps the spider trap prey. They kept records of web activity on a daily basis. It was found that honeybees did pay attention to the zigzags. If they got caught but escaped, they learned to avoid the pattern on the next trip from home to blossom. But a spider removes and respins a new web and a different pattern each morning, so with the pattern altered, even a knowing bee can blunder into the web.

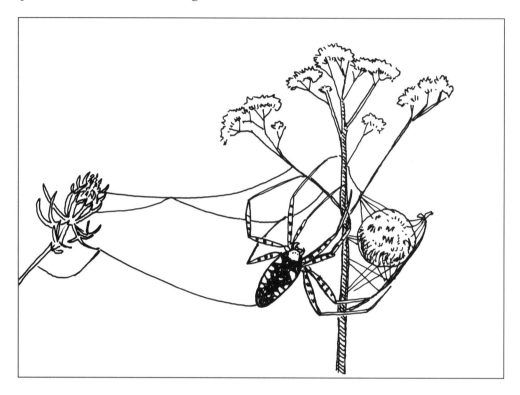

HOW TO FIND SPIDER WEBS

A web shining with morning dew or raindrops is the easiest to spot, but look along the edges of a field or between tall plant stems for the suspended pattern of a spider and its zigzag. Watch the behavior of bees that pass by. Do they seem to observe the web? Has the spider caught any insects that day? Look for small silk-wrapped bundles of prey in the web. In late summer search in nearby grass clusters for the silk-covered sphere of eggs. Make a sketch of the zigzag and return the next day to compare the shapes.

Plants Create a Field of Energy

Imagine your field without its cover of plants. During the day the energy of sunlight would fall on the bare soil, only to be reflected as light or absorbed as heat. During the dark hours the heat would dissipate and the energy would be lost. The plants that grow in your field capture the energy of sunlight, storing it as a bond between atoms of carbon, oxygen, and hydrogen, and then transport the energy, now turned to sugar, to places in the plant where cells are being made. The energy to build cells is released when the bonds are broken.

1 Turning Sunlight into Sugar and Passing It on

Materials:

- Paper
- Drawing materials

Background: All the creatures that feed on nectar, sap, or leaves capture some sugar energy to power their own growth and activity. After being eaten, the energy in the plant material keeps changing. Some energy from the sugar is used for movement or to maintain body heat. Some is used to create offspring. Even after death, there is energy stored in body tissues, and the decomposers move into the energy chain that began with sunlight on a leaf.

Procedure: As you explore your field and its borders, try to find examples of energy strands involving at least three steps. A butterfly feeding on a flower, for instance, would be the third step in a strand that starts with sunlight energy, transformed into nectar by the plant, then used by the butterfly in its life processes.

85

What might the fourth step of this strand look like? A labeled and illustrated chart might look like the following:

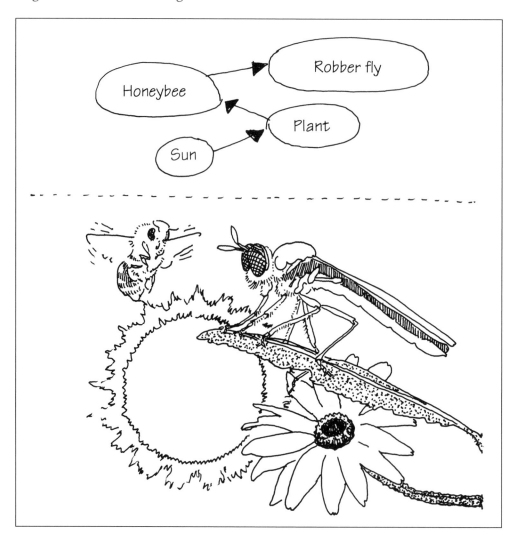

Try to find examples that include decomposers such as fungi, soil bacteria, and earthworms.

2 How Plants Make Food

Materials:

- Two plants of the same size and in pots of equal size. (Start seeds of your own or use two house plants of the same kind.)

Background: Sunshine helps a plant make food in the process called photosynthesis, Latin for "made with light." When sunlight shines on a green leaf (or stem), little green globs of chlorophyll are activated. Powered by energy from the sunlight, the chlorophyll is then able to break apart carbon dioxide (which has come in through the pores) and water (which has come in through the veins). The pieces of the water and gas molecules are then reassembled into a new shape—a sugar molecule.

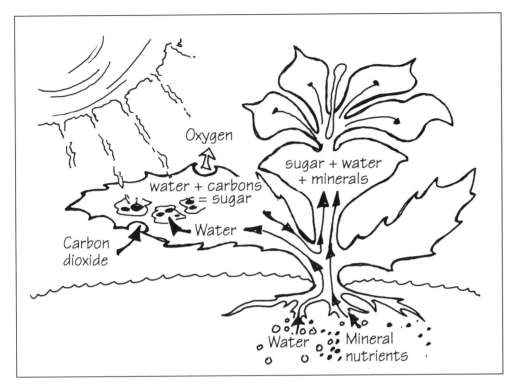

Light from the sun powers the sugar-making process inside the leaf. Water and carbon dioxide are used to assemble molecules of sugar. The sugar flows as sap to wherever the plant is growing. At the growth site, the sugar energy is used to create plant cells and essential chemicals and proteins. Water and nutrients, flowing up from the roots, are also used in the process.

Sugar can be written in chemical notation of atoms joined to make the molecule $C_6H_{12}O_6$, or six carbons, twelve hydrogens, and six oxygens. The atoms form a rigid pattern of partnerships held in place by sun energy, now in the form of a chemical bond. When the molecule is taken apart in the presence of oxygen (for instance, through cell metabolism), the bond is broken, the energy is released, and the atoms recombine into their original, simpler molecules of carbon dioxide and water, the waste products of all organic growth processes. The abundant life of the field is clear evidence of the effectiveness of the process.

Although you can't really observe the process of a leaf making sugar, you can observe a plant's response to light as an indication of how important light is to its life.

Procedure: As an experiment, grow one plant in a sunny window and another of the same size and species in a dark or shaded situation. You can use two house plants, or you can grow your own bean plants by starting dry soup beans in equal amounts of soil and in pots of the same size.

Put one plant on the windowsill and either cover the other plant with a dark container or put it in a sunless part of the room. Both plants will adjust their leaves so they can collect as much light as possible, but the shaded plant will put most of its energy into growing toward any source of light. What other differences do you notice? Are there differences in the size or color of the leaf? Does one plant need more water than the other? (The plant in the light should be photosynthesizing more and thus using more water.) If possible, continue growing the plants until they make flowers and beans. Which plant makes flowers, the most seeds, that is, offspring?

3 Adaptations of Leaves That Live in the Open

Materials:

- An expendable plant that has been living inside (perhaps a bean plant from the preceding activity)

Background: On a summer's day in the open field, the life-giving sunshine can also cause extreme stress to an exposed plant. A plant cannot choose to photosynthe-size—whenever light hits the leaf, the sugar-making process begins spontaneously. Carbon dioxide and water flow in, and sugars and oxygen flow out. The larger the leaf, the more sugar can be made. Only one other variable is necessary: water, which must be abundant and accessible. Unless the field borders a wetland, water in the field habitat is often limited. The plants that survive there often show modifications that limit water loss. Look for some of the following adaptations in the plants in your study area:

Mullein leaves grow in a low rosette and have white fuzzy leaves.

- Narrow, upright leaves capture the gentler sunlight of mornings and afternoons, avoiding the drying heat of noon.

- Leaves growing in clusters or dense tufts shade their own roots and may form a moisture-saving mulch with last year's leaves.

- Fuzzy or waxy surfaces on leaves, stems, and buds help shade the plant or reduce evaporation from intense radiation.

Procedure: If you have finished the preceding experiment with bean plants or have an extra plant, place it outside during sunny, mild weather. How does the bean plant respond to midday radiation? (A bean plant will either raise its leaves to an upright position or, if the radiation doesn't help, wilt.)

Pollination

Flowers provide a fascinating study of an ongoing and mutually beneficial relationship between plants and their pollinators. Many insects are totally dependent on the pollen and nectar that plants provide, and the plants are totally dependent on the particular insects, birds, and sometimes bats that move their pollen and fertilize their seeds.

4 **What Insects Get from Plants**

Materials:

- Pen or pencil
- Notebook or paper and clipboard

Background: If you are exploring during the growing season, look for flowers. What is it about the flower that catches *your* attention? Blur your vision by squinting and look over the field. Do the bright colors distinguish the flowers from the background of leaves? Or is it something about the flowers' shapes? The attributes that catch the human eye have actually evolved to attract the attention of pollinating insects. The following activities will help you see some of the dynamics of the relationship between plants and insect pollinators.

Procedure: Take a sketching pad or notebook to the field when flowers are blooming. Choose one flower to observe closely and watch what an insect does as it approaches and lands on that flower. (*Note:* Bees and wasps will sting when defending their nest but will rarely react defensively when visiting flowers—use reasonable caution and respect when observing them.) The insect's goal is food, and it will move quickly and efficiently to get it. The food may be the sugary, energy-rich nectar or it may be the pollen, a source of protein usually sought as food for the growing larvae back home. Make a sketch of the insects you observe to help you identify them later. Record what the insect collects and what part of the plant it visits. (Nectar is usually located deep within the flower; pollen is usually more on the outskirts of the petals.)

5 What Plants Get from Insects

Materials:

- Pen or pencil
- Notebook or paper and clipboard

Background: As an insect goes from flower to flower collecting food, its movements distribute pollen over the surface of each flower. Pollination occurs only when the pollen falls on the tip of the central pistil and the pollen grains are stimulated to enter the pistil, which contains the unfertilized seeds or ovules. When the genes of the pollen and the genes of the ovules combine, the seeds are said to be fertile, able to grow into new individuals. An insect is busy collecting food for itself or its young, and it usually works on just the flowers it knows are producing pollen or nectar. There is a tendency for insects to visit only one species of flower, a habit that promotes cross-pollination (pollen getting moved between flowers of separate plants of the same species).

Procedure: Check it out. *Do* bees, butterflies, and wasps tend to visit the same species of flowering plants, or do they visit whichever flowers are near? (Mixed pollens might not be very effective in pollinating flowers.) Choose a field or garden with a variety of blooming plants. Try to follow one insect on its rounds. Note the sequence of flowers it visits. (If you don't know the names, use some notation, such as Flower A, B, or C.)

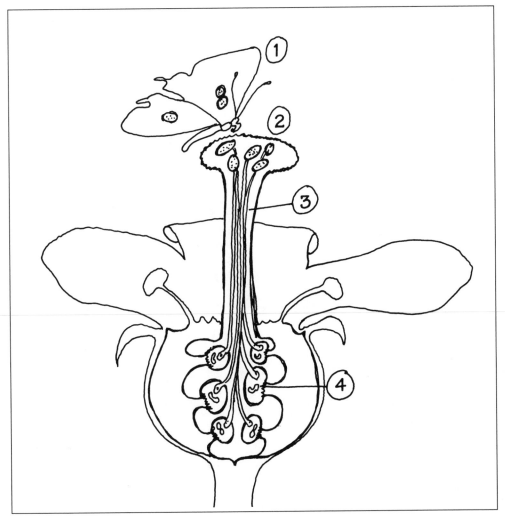

1. Visitor brings pollen.

2. Pollen on the stigma tip is stimulated to grow thin tubes down into the flower's ovary.

3. Each tube seeks out an unfertilized ovule. Sperm move down the pollen tube into the ovule.

4. The ovule is now a fertile seed and begins to develop into a tiny plant, encased in a protective seed coat.

Looking for Genetic Variation

Some flowers can self-pollinate without needing insects to cross-pollinate their flowers, but the offspring of self-pollinated flowers all resemble that one parent. What's the problem in producing identical offspring? Seeds formed as the result of genetic mixing have better chances, over many generations, of coping with environmental changes. And the changes always occur. We know from studies of ancient rocks, fossils, and soils that continents shift, climates warm and cool, land rises and sinks. If the genes that make up a species can be represented by a wide range of forms and responses, then, whatever the change, some members of the species might survive to carry the genetic heritage into the future.

6 Flowers as Signs and Signals—A Pollinator's Treasure Hunt

Materials:

- Pen or pencil
- Blank notebook page or a copy of the following procedure section

Background: If you have observed insects on a variety of blossoms, you will have noticed that the food-collecting behavior depends on the shape of the flower. The flowers of goldenrod and Queen Anne's lace offer a wide landing platform on which many insects feed freely. Tubelike flowers, such as jewelweeds, restrict entry to individuals of a certain shape or size of mouthparts. Only the tongues of bumblebees or hummingbirds are able to reach the nectar hidden down the crooked pocket in the back of the jewelweed flower. As they visit successive jewelweeds in search of nectar, both those creatures are the right size to pick up and deposit pollen. A close fit between flower and pollinator means a neat exchange of services: The pollinator is given exclusive access to food, and the plant gets a more precise transfer of pollen.

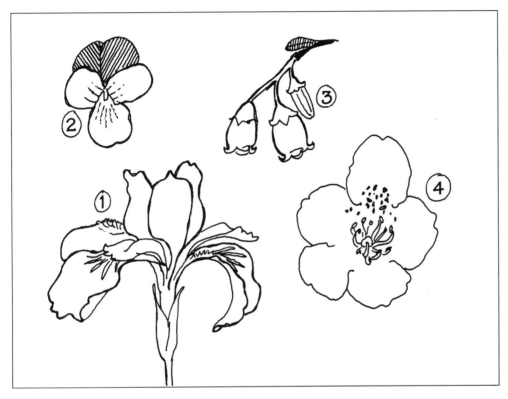

Many flowers have evolved designs and shapes that help insects locate the pollen or nectar they seek.

1. Converging lines.

2. Contrasting colors.

3. Handholds

4. Dots that position the insect for finding nectar.

Procedure: Make drawings of some of the flowers you see showing the structures that plants have evolved in their relationship with pollinators. Look for examples of each of the following:

1. Find an insect-pollinated flower that has some signal that operates over a wide range (a bright color or strong scent) and which may alert insects to its presence.

2. As the insect flies closer to investigate, it will seek to land and search for food. Find a flower with strong colors and patterns that converge at the site of the nectar or pollen. You will probably notice some dots, converging lines, or contrasting central bull's-eye pattern that accentuate the location of the food.

3. Find a flower with a shape that might help direct the pollinator's movements. Look for structures that might serve to funnel the insect. Notches in the petals that might serve as footholds or broad petals that look like landing fields might help direct the insect's body to face the best food sources.

4. Find a flower that is choosy. Petal doors or sticky hairs may block out too-large visitors. The right-sized visitor will deposit pollen as it enters and pick up a new pollen dusting on the way out; a creature that is too large or too small may not put the pollen in the right place.

7 Being a Bee

Materials:

- Small sticks (toothpicks or pipe cleaners will also work)
- Cotton ball
- Single open blossoms or clustered flowers

Procedure: Observe some pollinating insects working the blossoms. Notice their angle of approach and their behavior when they land and leave. Try to design some model pollinators, using toothpicks and cotton. Twist tufts of cotton around a toothpick until the cotton is the size of the pollinator's body. Then "fly" your model onto the flower (head toward the nectar guides) and observe how pollen is deposited on the model. Try again on another blossom of the same species to see how the pollen might get rubbed off on the stigma's surface. This activity will be most effective using large, single flowers such as jewelweed, lilies, daffodils, or rhododendrons.

Some flowers are open to all pollinators. This thistle is made up of a bunch of small blossoms, each able to produce its own seed. The fluffy seeds at the top are ripe and ready to leave.

Plants on the Move, Plants Settled Down

The insects are not the only small winged things on the move in a meadow. While watching for bees and butterflies, your eye may be caught by seeds blown by the wind.

8 Flying Seeds

Materials:

- A net might be fun to use to catch winged seeds in the air, but hands will do the job.

  Note: Choose a day in late spring or late summer when you know fluffy seeds are out.

Background: Many seeds are attached to some sort of parachute or winglike device that slows their descent enough so that air currents can take them well away from their origins. Why away? The place where the parent is growing must be ideal—why not just drop the seeds there?

The seed receives a food packet from the parent plant, which helps it get started, but its best hope for future growth is away from the soil the parent has already used for its growth and away from the shade it makes. To compete with an already established plant would be too difficult; the best bet is a new site. But, unlike animals, individual plants cannot uproot and traipse off. Winged seeds, though, can travel on the wind.

Procedure: Capture some seeds and try to track them back to their parent plants. Most of the parents will be nonwoody field plants such as milkweed, dandelion, and

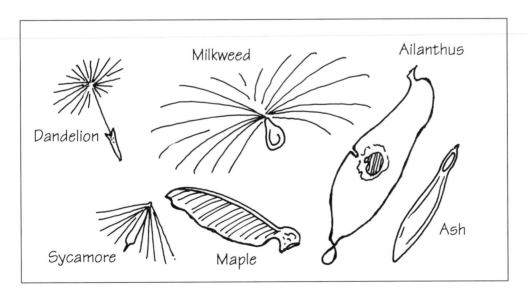

goldenrod, but check out nearby maples, pines, sycamores, ashes, and ailanthus or other sources of seeds.

Most wind-carried tree seeds require sunlight for germination and continued light for growth. Such plants are often the first colonizers of an unmowed field. If they grow untouched by fire, grazing animals, or mowers, they transform the field into woodland.

9 Hitchhiking Seeds

Materials:

- A large disposable pair of old socks to wear over shoes, bare legs, or pants.

Background and Procedure: Some plants solve the problem of distribution to new sites by producing seeds that hitch a ride with other inhabitants of the ecosystem. Berries, for example, are gathered or eaten by birds and mice. Forgotten caches or defecated seeds then can grow in new sites.

The burrs you find on your socks or a dog's fur are seed travelers too. Sticky seeds, such as burrdock, tick-trefoil, and beggar's ticks, are very likely to get caught in the fur of animals on their way through the field. Eventually the animal will be bothered by the mat of burrs and will stop to chew out the mess. In the process, the seeds drop out. If the grooming takes place on the edge of the path or on the mound of earth at the animal's burrow, the seeds will fall on a perfect site: disturbed soil, near where animals are likely to pass to pick up burrs.

You can imitate the way furry animals help some seeds find new sites to grow. Try wearing old socks or stockings over your shoes, legs, or pants to make collecting (and disposal) easier. Then take a walk through a field in the late summer or fall. Check your coverings frequently to find out which sections of the field have the most burr-producing plants.

10 Identifying Plant Colonies

Materials:

- Drawing materials

Background: As you explore the field and edge area, you may notice that some places have lots of the same kind of plant. The clustering might be the result of the success of many seedlings, as seen in Activity 13 (page 102), but it may also be the colonizing of one successful plant. A colony will most likely have larger, older plants in the center with smaller plants on the fringe.

There are two basic ways that a plant species can expand into an area rich in the resources it needs. Once established in a good place to grow, some species grow more stems or roots out from their bases, creating thick bunches, or tussocks. Grasses are especially good at this strategy: Their thick stems and roots eventually form a dense mat which crowds out any weaker plants. One grass called broom or buffalo grass (*Andropogon* sp.) secretes poisons through its roots that kill the competition. Other kinds of plants send out special stems, or runners, over the surface of the soil (crab grass, clover); some runners travel just under the soil (witch grass, Canada goldenrod, sumac, milkweed), and others grow long canes that root at the tip where the cane touches the ground (blackberry, raspberry, osiers).

The larger trunks in this sumac colony are those of the oldest plants. The smaller plants on the outer edge are the "branches" of those same plants, sent up from underground runners.

Procedure: By making a drawing of something, you can often see new aspects because you have looked more closely at its form. Find several examples of plant colonization and make diagrams of the pattern of growth. A diagram doesn't show all the leaves and stems, but it should show the relative heights of the stems and the general position of the leaves. Try to find several different strategies to represent. If you are working in a group, compare your drawings for similar patterns or trade sketches and try to find the species by looking at the diagrams.

The Field Habitat in Transition

If a field area is unmowed, ungrazed, and free from fire for several seasons, the habitat will eventually change. The area filled with grasses will be grown over by shrubs and vines. Sapling trees, sprouting on the shaded soil, will grow up through the shrubs. Eventually, the shrubs are shaded out and die. As the plant community changes, so does the animal community. This successive change of plants and animals is a natural process: Any living thing eventually alters the system that supports it. That change, in turn, creates habitats for new species.

The hardy shrubs that are able to grow in the open field create a more moderate environment under their branches. These protected areas can be the perfect place for young trees to sprout and grow.

11 Field Surveys: Looking for Evidence of Future Changes

Field Survey A

Background: If left to develop naturally, fields are always in the process of becoming woodland. Unmowed meadow grasses provide the perfect environment for woody shrubs, brambles, and young trees to take seed. With their stronger roots and taller stems, the woody plants begin to overpower the grasses and herbs. The varying proportions of woody plants to meadow plants will determine the kinds of animals you will find in a field. Each insect, bird, and furred or scaly creature has special requirements of space, light, and plant growth. These are the elements that decide its placement, or niche, in the ecosystem. With each seasonal change and each year's cycle, the makeup of plants and animals in the field is altered, and new patterns of relationships overlay and overcome the older matrix.

Procedure: Look for young specimens of woody plants in your study area. At first the invading saplings of trees and shrubs may be difficult to distinguish from the nonwoody (herbaceous) plants of the same size. As you look carefully, though, you will find that the stems of woody plants have a different character: The wood of a young tree stem is more flexible than that of a goldenrod, for instance, and the leaves are larger higher up from the ground. A sapling is also more likely to start at its base as a single stem and then fork into side branches, while the herbaceous plants tend to grow as clumps of single stalks.

Keep a descriptive list of the invaders you find, perhaps including leaf samples to help in identification. You probably won't find more than five or six different species in your study area. Check your library for identification guides to trees and shrubs; Symond's books have excellent photographs.

Field Survey B

Background: In many fields, the plants on the outer edges of the field are denser, shrubbier and woodier than the woody plants you found within the field. Perhaps the mower can't cut them down because of fences or ditches, or perhaps the field is bordered by a woodland or wetland where the mower can't go. As you explore your area, you will find that this border zone is rich in species diversity. Protected from mowing, but open to the sun, plants grow abundantly on the border. Here mammals hide and hunt and insects find food shelter.

Procedure: Look in the border or in a nearby woodland for specimens of plants that match the ones you found out in the field. Which ones are found in both places? What differences do you notice in their sizes or shapes? How would you explain the differences? (Age, crowding, shade from a nearby forest?) Describe and sketch the plants you find and try to find out what their names are.

Needs and Niches

By following seeds and searching for offspring, you can see how each plant generation gets dispersed. The dispersal process is somewhat random; many seeds land in unfavorable locations. If enough seeds are launched, at least some will end up in areas suitable for their needs. Success depends on the seedling's opportunity to grow toward the light and find nutrients and water in the soil. If it succeeds, it will flower and set seed. The conditions that support those requirements of each species make up its niche.

12 Measuring Plant Diversity

Materials:

- Notebook and pen or pencil
- A yardstick or a straight stick with equal units marked at about 6-inch (10-cm) intervals

Background: As you look over a field, you will notice that the distribution of species varies; a particular plant may grow abundantly in one area and be absent in another. Its niche, its place of abundance, includes not only the soil and water conditions, but its relation to the animals and the other plants of its environment.

Procedure: A yardstick (or marked stick about the same length) makes a good device for comparing the diversity of plant species in different areas of the field. You may wish to measure the abundance of a particular kind of plant, or you may want to compare areas that appear different (or the same). Lay the stick down close to the soil and count the number of different species of plants touching the edge. You might repeat the procedure three times and average the numbers. To compare areas, repeat your procedure in other parts of the field, especially in areas that seem different to you.

In what ways do you think soil moisture, sunlight, or organic material in the soil relates to the comparisons you recorded? Which combination of characteristics supports the greatest diversity of species—that is, the greatest number of niches?

Sample data sheet:

Site number and location	General description of soil makeup (texture and moisture content)	Daily exposure to sunlight (full, partial, shade)	Numbers of different species per measure or Number of a particular species per measure

Strategic Alliances: Ants and Aphids

Some relationships have evolved to the point where two or several species are allies, each benefiting the other directly. A female aphid, for example, can establish herself on a plant in early summer and begin a colonizing process, giving birth to live young (all females, exactly like the mother). The aphid family forms a dense colony on plants and leaves, sucking sugary sap through their hollow mouth tubes.

Alliances may be formed with ants who protect the little herd of aphids from predators. By grooming the aphids, the ants extract concentrated sugar from special glands in the aphids. Later in the growing season, winged forms of aphids are produced. The winged ones disperse, sometimes to a different species of food plant, depending on the species of aphid. Just as the cold season approaches, the adult females give birth to males. They mate with the females, and fertile eggs are laid. The eggs will survive the cold and drought that kills the adult aphids. Ants may carry some of the aphids underground where they spend the winter in special chambers. When summer returns, the aphids are brought to the surface and placed on plants to form their herds once more.

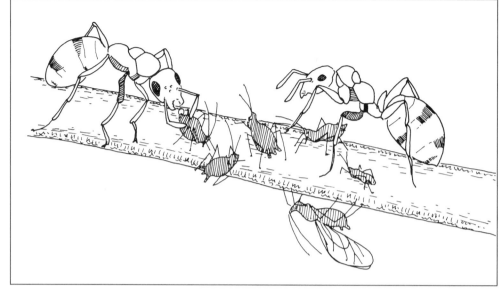

Ants tend the aphids, stroking them to extract extra sugar fluid. Ladybug beetles and their larva may try to eat the aphids but would be driven off by the biting ants.

Look along flower stalks or tender woody tree stems for clusters of aphids. Use a magnifying glass to observe their various sizes. Try to find their predators, perhaps lacewing larva hiding in the herd. Watch out for the guarding ants; they will attack you as a threat to their herd.

13 Looking for Clues of Alliances and Interactions

Background and Procedure: You can get an idea of which plants and animals interact by looking for signs of their activities. Look for any variation of symmetry in a leaf or a chewed end of stem. Creatures that travel frequently through the grass often leave paths. Routes that prove safe are reused and become clear, well-worn paths as animals repeatedly travel along them from shelter to dependable food sources.

In a sense, a path is a kind of energy-saving device—by using a known path, an animal can spend its energy getting food instead of finding its way. Look especially along the edges of the field since many creatures will travel or live in the cover of longer grass or shrubs, using a path to enter the field, then moving more randomly through the field in search of seasonal foods. As you move about exploring the field, pay attention to how it feels to you to be walking through a pathless area and then to move through a place on a path.

14 Meadow Mouse Signs

Materials:

- Plywood or wooden planks to cover at least an area three feet square (cardboard can be used if it is weighted down on the edges)

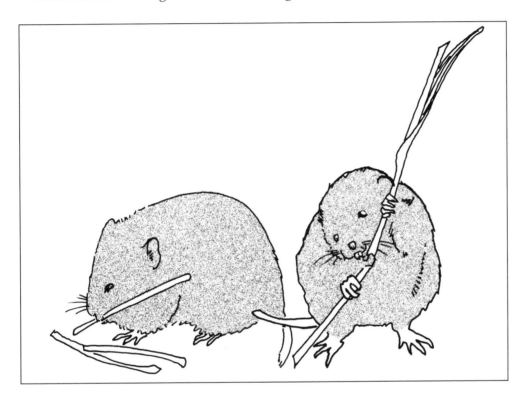

Background: Voles, or meadow mice, are usually the most numerous mammals in a field and can create a crisscrossing network of paths throughout the area. They will make a path by butting and pushing up the layer of old grass thatch, making neat little covered tunnels about the same width as a school ruler. (They can also tunnel through the soil to get at bulbs and roots. Much of the damage to garden plants attributed to moles is actually done by meadow mice.) If you can follow some tunnels, you may come across a collection of harvested grass stems, cut to the length of matches, or a path that dead-ends in a pile of mouse droppings—the toilet area. You may also find a mound of soft grasses the size of a softball, the nursery nest for baby voles.

Procedure: You will be able to see vole construction patterns very well if you leave a large piece of plywood or several planks flat on the ground, especially in a spot where you have already seen some vole tunnels. After a week or so, peek under carefully; voles seek out protective cover for nesting and food storage. You may also see a number of the soil-dwelling creatures discussed in the chapter on worn zones, such as sowbugs, centipedes, millipedes, and shiny black ground beetles.

15 Requirements for Healthy Habitats

Materials:

- Town map

Background: Vole nests and babies can be found throughout the growing season when there is plenty of grass to feed them. Mother meadow mice can produce four or five young every few weeks. The mouse population is usually kept in check by a variety of predators: hawks, crows, owls, foxes, coyotes, snakes, and raccoons. In places where these animals are scarce, the voles' readiness to breed and eat can result in a population overflow, a depleted food supply, and an ecosystem out of whack. In one intensive study, it was found that when coyotes stopped hunting in an area because of too much development, the meadow mouse population rose and, since mice are carnivorous if the prey is defenseless, as the vole population rose there was increased loss of baby songbirds. Lots of hungry mice eventually consumed the food supply, and many voles left in search of new habitats. But in areas where roads and house lots broke up the previously continuous field and shrub land, most migrating mice died of starvation or were killed by cars or house cats.

We can understand fairly easily, how an energy network functions, how the loss of a link, a common food plant perhaps, can break the strand. The loss of that one plant species would mean the loss of every creature that depended on the plant. Any animals or plants that depended on these creatures would also be affected.

The damage can eventually be repaired if another field habitat is close enough for reseeding to occur. In many areas of the world, however, there has been too much fragmentation of the original habitats that had evolved to fit and use the resources of the area. We have assumed, in the past, that if we could just provide protection for small sanctuaries, then we could alter the rest of the environment as we wished. We are finding out that our environment works as an integrated system; it functions poorly if its parts are isolated. We are learning that the balance of one habitat often depends on another area that may at first seem unconnected. Each serves as a kind of backup system to recharge any breakdown in the life strands of the others.

Procedure: Check your town map for examples of fields and open areas that are set aside as wild lands. Could animals or plants move easily from one protected area to another? Visit several areas and try to figure out if the fields have the same kinds of plants and animals living in them. If one area lost a particular species of plant, for instance, could it be seeded in from nearby habitats?

Find examples of other fields in your area. (Check your town map for pre-served open land.) Look for paths and clues and try to figure out if they have the same kinds of plants and animals living there. Could the animals move into your study site? (Roadways or rivers may block the way.) If your study site lost a particular species of plant, could it be seeded in from other fields?

Do you find any animals that you know use habitats other than fields and borders? For instance, do any of the birds migrate elsewhere during cold weather? Do any of the amphibians use distant ponds for breeding? Do any of the mammals that feed in the field raise their young in the protection of the forest? Explore other habitats in your area for evidence of connections.

16 How Do Butterflies Help Ecologists?

Materials:

- Field guide to butterflies
- Paper and pen or pencil

Background: A balanced ecosystem means that there are many strands of lives through which energy can pass. With their specific tastes and short life cycles, butterflies are good indicators of ecological diversity. Ecologists have been able to recreate miniature prairies by carefully reseeding open land with native prairie plants. But if native butterflies are reintroduced and do not survive, some important link in the strand must be missing; only a complete ecosystem can support butterflies.

Chrysalids collected in early summer may hatch out for a late summer generation of butterflies. Each should be carefully and firmly supported so that the hatching butterfly will have room to spread its wings. Check frequently for newly emerged butterflies and release them as soon as they can fly.

Procedure: Since butterfly larvae are usually very picky eaters, you can learn to find caterpillars by searching for their favorite food plants during the summer months. Read about the requirements and seasonal cycles of particular butterflies, then read what their favorite plants look like and where they live. Once you have found the caterpillar, record what you notice about which parts of the plant it eats and any changes you observe as the caterpillar grows. Just before it pupates, the caterpillar will go into a wandering phase. When it finds the right conditions, it will change into a pupa. If the butterfly goes through two life cycles (the larva and the pupa) per summer, the early pupa will soon hatch as a butterfly. Late-summer pupa will pupate all winter. Butterflies vary, so read up on the ones you are interested in.

17 Establishing a Claim: The Field's Resources

Materials:

- Pen or pencil
- Carefully drawn map of the study site area
- Bird identification guide
- Binoculars (optional)

Background: If you hear a bird singing as you move around the field, try to locate and identify it. If you can comfortably sit and watch for a while, you may see it fly to sing from several perches. Although a bird has many predators and must keep near sheltering grass or branches, it usually sings from a prominent perch from which it can see and be seen and heard. The perches are generally located on the edges of its territory, its "yard," from which it chases away other birds of its species. The singing notifies other birds of its aggressive intentions. The same songs often attract female birds who, on checking out the territory for potential nesting and feeding sites, may offer themselves as a mate to the singing male and, in some species, join him in singing the boundaries.

The situation is something like boundary disputes among nations. As long as the location of the boundary is uncertain, fighting and bloodshed are likely to occur; an established boundary results in less warring. In a very real sense, birds are saving energy by not having to fight each time they meet.

Procedure: Try to figure out the respective territories of some prominently singing bird species for your area. If you see a bird chasing another of its species, watch where the chase lets up. If this marks the beginning of the second bird's territory, it may swing around and chase back the first bird. Where neither bird will budge, the

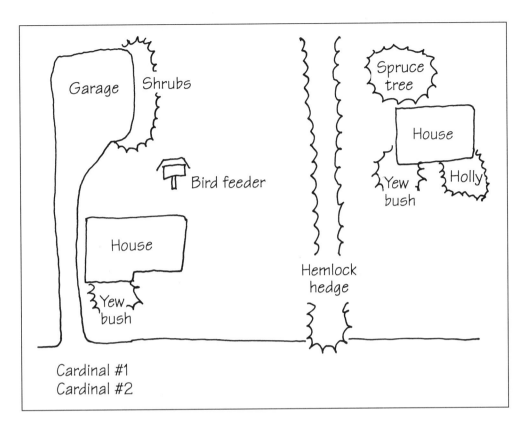

Garage   Shrubs

Spruce
tree

House

Yew
bush   Holly

Bird feeder

House

Hemlock
hedge

Yew
bush

Cardinal #1
Cardinal #2

territorial boundary will form. If something happens to either bird so that the singing and chasing stops, each territory is up for grabs. A nesting bird's territory will include singing perches, feeding areas, and a nesting site. Try to locate and label areas that have special uses. Birds that sing loudly and are common will be the easiest to track. Consider song sparrows, robins, starlings, redwing blackbirds, or mockingbirds. While the first four species make exclusive territories only during the breeding season, mockingbirds sing their territories all year round. (The males and females will have separate zones during the winter months.)

Other Animal Signs and Messages

Many creatures, from crickets to coyotes, have some means of designating an area as a territory they are willing to defend. Like singing, territorial markers warn interlopers and forestall serious fights. Ecologists learn a great deal about the life of a creature by studying its territorial behavior. The kinds of places an animal chooses reflects its needs for food and shelter, and by comparing territories, an observer can compare the needs of different animals.

Mammals, with their keen sense of smell, are able to leave scent messages along paths or in prominent places to indicate the boundaries of their territory. The odors of their excrement are personal signatures, apparently, and many mammals add secretions from glands located on either side of the anus. Dogs have scent glands between their toe pads—you may have seen dogs scrape the ground vigorously with their hind legs after marking a spot with their urine.

If you are familiar with dog habits of frequent marking with urine, you can easily imagine marking behavior of coyotes and foxes. Male canids (dogs, wolves, coyotes, foxes, etc.) often use prominent features as marking posts and "message centers." Fox markings, especially, have a slightly skunky smell that makes them distinctive to human noses. A fox's boundary marking will be noticed in only a small area, while the odor of a frightened skunk will be noticeable over a large area. (Since the skunk's principal predator is the great horned owl, a strong skunk odor at the base of a large tree might indicate an owl nest above.)

18 Strands of Interrelationships: Making an Energy-Transfer Diagram

Materials:

- Paper
- Pen or pencil

Background and Procedure: To show how energy moves from one group of field organisms to the next, make a diagram showing the plants and animals you have found. To begin, make groupings of the names of the field and edge organisms, starting with the rarest group—the predators of other animals. Your list of large hunters will probably be short; it is unusual to see a hawk flying over or to glimpse a fox on a hunt. The smaller insect-eaters, such as snakes, spiders, flycatchers, and other birds, will probably be the more common predators.

Next, list the creatures in your field that are hunted—the species of plant-eating birds, small mammals, and insects. Prey animals are usually more abundant and in greater variety than their predators. In even larger numbers are the plants that feed the plant-eaters. You may not have been able to learn all their names, but you can describe or draw them to represent their diversity on your list. Include the sunlight in your diagram as the initial source of all energy.

Look for relationships between species in your groupings. Draw straight lines between any organisms that share a predator-prey relationship. Draw dotted lines between any organisms that relate in terms of shelter, nesting material, or other structural need. As one organism eats another, the prey's body is turned into energy.

By looking at the diagram of energy strands formed by your lists of field inhabitants, you can see how the ecosystem's energy network takes the shape of a huge gumdrop: Its base is sunlight which provides energy for the large number of primary producers, which pass their energy on to the plant-eaters whose sugars and proteins eventually become the sinews and blood of a sparrow hawk or a fox. Most

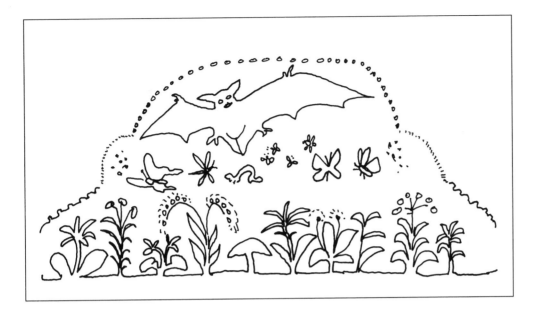

of the energy is lost by the processes of living and growing so there is not much sun-energy available for meat-eaters; six-sevenths of the energy mass is lost with each transfer from the one eaten to the one who eats. The small group at the top of your gumdrop diagram is an accurate reflection of the dynamics of energy transfer in a natural ecosystem.

Human Use of Energy Resources

If you've ever taken a ride in an airplane, you no doubt have observed the many ways the landscape has been transformed for human use. Even a walk through a city, suburb, or farming area reveals constant evidence of how people use the planet's energy for food, transportation, and manufacturing processes. Humans have a monopoly on the earth's resources and have certainly benefited from this position, but we are beginning to see the problems in our procedures.

19 How Do We Get What We Need?

Materials:

- Paper for writing
- Pen or pencil

Background: Many people do not fully grasp the complexity of the energy systems that support our lives. It is easier for us to understand the needs of our culture than it is to grasp the importance of water cycles or insect predators. If any species is to continue, it must fit into the pattern of flow of available energy. Too many voles creates a serious problem, but so do too many coyotes. The network is delicately intricate, and the energy, the resources on which all must live, is always limited.

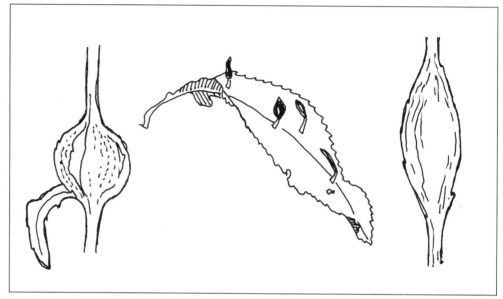

Gall makers are examples of organisms that live without destroying their life-support systems. *Left to right:* Goldenrod ball gall, made by a fly; cherry leaf galls, made by mites; elliptical goldenrod gall, made by a moth.

Procedure: Start to think about what your resources are. What must you have to live and grow? Begin by listing any food you have used today. Select several different items and list the events that brought these foods to you. If you ate berries that were growing outside your door, then you were living close to your local ecosystem, consuming energy that was just one step away from being sunlight. But if the berries were in jam that came from the store, a great deal more energy was required to get the berry into you.

Consider all the steps you can think of: the trip from the field to the processing plant, the jam-making process, the sugar and glass (and all their processing steps), the use of gasoline in getting the jar to the store, your trip to the store, and your toasting of bread to put under the jelly. Your berry-jelly connection may constitute a very large and far-flung ecosystem. In terms of energy costs, most humans in North America have ecosystems that are very expensive to maintain and very fragile.

Our extravagant use of energy resouces is the greatest the earth has ever witnessed. Until just a few generations ago, people weren't even capable of using so much energy to make things, get around, or keep comfortable. Basically, we had only sunlight and wood for fuel (or ancient plant products such as coal or oil). As we began making electricity and processing petroleum, the dangers of using so much energy were unknown or overlooked. Some smoke and a few dead fish seemed a small price to pay for the convenience of increased energy. Besides, some people were getting rich from the proceeds.

In order to refine oil into the gasoline that powers our cars and trucks, in order to make the electricity that warms our water, our buildings, and drives our appliances, we create waste materials that can be extremely toxic to life. Not only are we using up resources that cannot be replenished (oil and coal are fossilized plant products in limited supply), but the waste products are new problems in themselves. The use of radioactive materials to make electricity results in a byproduct that is impossible to dispose of safely. Radioactive wastes are so deadly that we rate their toxicity in thousands of years.

In natural ecosystems sun energy is limited, available only during the daylight hours. But we can turn on the electric lights whenever we wish, and since the electricity that comes into our homes is not restricted, it is difficult to think of it as a limited resource or to remember that a light left on means that fuel is being burned somewhere. Since some people make money when lights are left on and since it costs corporations money to reduce their pollution, it is really up to the energy users to cut back on energy overuse.

Your first step in sensitizing yourself to saving energy is to list all the ways you use it and decide on which ones you can do without. It might help to talk with other people to find out what energy-saving alternatives they have discovered. Several books listed in the bibliography offer good ideas. You may find that the satisfaction of cutting back and knowing that you are helping will outweigh the small inconvenience of learning new behaviors.

20 Reading an Electric Meter

Materials:

- A copy of the worksheet below or a facsimile drawing

- Pen or pencil

Background: The building you live in already has a device for measuring the electricity your family uses. The electric meter may be in the basement or outside. Within the glass case are several dials, each with a single hand marking a point on a face of numbers, one to ten. The dials are read by recording the number indicated on each moving left to right. The resulting number is a measure of kilowatt-hours. (A 100-watt light bulb uses 100 watt-hours of energy in one hour of burning. A kilowatt-hour is equal to 1,000 watt-hours—what you would use if you left 10 100-watt bulbs on for an hour.) When the electric company's meter-reader comes to record

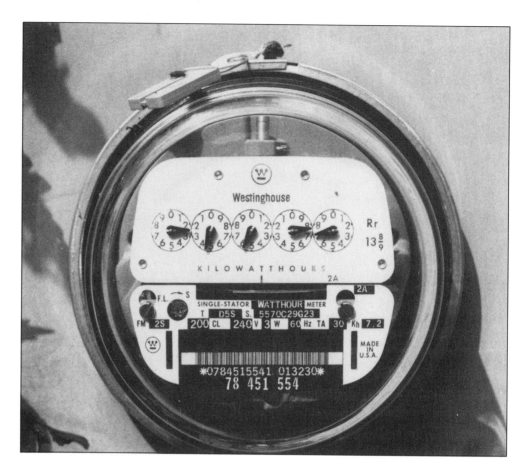

your family's monthly electricity use, last month's number will be subtracted from this month's number and you will be billed accordingly.

Procedure: To get some idea of which activities use the most electricity in your home, record the numbers on the meter before and after the electrical equipment is used. (The water heater will be working to replace used hot water *after* the shower or washing machine has finished, so allow for heating time in your records.)

Choose three different time periods that represent your family's normal weekly activities. Record the time (one hour each period) and the activities that used energy such as TV watching, showers, clothes or dish washing. (If your house uses electricity to heat water, your main energy use will be after the activity is done, when the water heater is working to heat the water that has refilled the hot water tank.) You can figure out which period and activities used the most energy by recording the numbers on each dial at the beginning and end of each time period. Your total energy used can be figured by subtracting the first number from the second. Use the setup on the next page to help organize your information.

Periods (Day of the week and beginning and ending times)	Activities	Dial numbers (Beginning–End)	Total energy used (in kilowatt-hours)

21 How We Can Cut Back on Our Energy Use

Materials:

- Two equal-sized pots, one with a lid (or one lidded pot and a watch with a second hand to time two separate experiments
- Equal amounts of water for two experiments

Background: Most environmentalists figure that we can still keep our homes safely lit and ourselves warm and well-fed by using energy only when it is needed and by using products that do not waste energy. Begin to act as though an alarm is sounding every time there is an unnecessary use of power for lighting, heating, and cooling your home. Little things count. If one 100-watt light bulb were left on for a year (is a night light left on every night?), it would cost us 400 pounds of nonrenewable coal to make the electricity and a heavy dose of air-polluting gases.

Procedure: Try the following experiment to see how a habit can misuse or save energy. Put equal amounts of water in equal-sized pots or saucepans. Put a lid on one pot, then heat them both until the water begins to boil in one. Which one will boil first? Which uses the least energy to get the job done?

Try out some of the following suggestions for cutting back on energy waste and the resulting pollution. Some suggestions you can use right away, every day, and save your family money. Others may call for expenditures for new products, but since they save energy, they will also result in long-term monetary and environmental savings.

- Turn out lights when you leave the room and use minimal lighting when you need it.
- Use hot water only when necessary. Take shorter hot showers; use cold water set-

tings for clothes; turn down the water heater thermostat to 120° F or less; let the dishes in the dishwasher air dry when the wash cycle is done.

- If you feel chilly inside your home, put on a sweater instead of turning up the thermostat.

- Try to minimize your appliance use. Could a broom or carpet sweeper do the job instead of the vacuum cleaner? Wouldn't a simple tool and some personal energy work just as well as the electric can opener, knife sharpener, electric mixer, or hair dryer?

- Do you have to use the clothes dryer? Most houses are dry enough in winter to dry clothes overnight on a folding rack, and sun-dried clothes and sheets in the summer have a smell that fabric softeners cannot duplicate. Consider not ironing slightly wrinkled items.

- Some appliances save energy. Use microwave ovens and toaster ovens instead of larger stove ovens whenever possible.

- Aluminum is our most energy-expensive metal to make. Recycle all aluminum, such as cans, pie pans, bakery-good trays, and foil.

- Try to plan your car trips to minimize its use. Grocery shop only once a week, and try to do several errands every time the car is used.

- Make your excursions to the refrigerator and freezer as brief as possible. Lots of cold air falls out when the door is open, and the refrigerater must use energy to replace the cold air. Turn the setting dial as warm as you can without making the ice cream soft.

- Add an insulating "vest" to your hot water heater to keep the heat in the tank. Most hardware stores have kits that are inexpensive and easy to install.

- Replace standard incandescent light bulbs with compact fluorescent bulbs (you may also need larger shades). Fluorescents use one-quarter the electricity of regular incandescent bulbs, which translates to a huge saving since nationally we use 25 percent of all energy for lighting and another 20 percent to make the electricity for lighting. If you are in school, present a case to your classmantes on how energy savings means money saved. The savings in a large home or public building can be tremendous. A school can save thousands of dollars just by replacing the bulbs that have to light up the exit signs.

- Find out all you can on alternatives to burning fossil fuels to make energy. Find out about making electricity with wind-powered generators, solar power and storage systems, converting wastes into methane gas, electric cars, improved public transportation, and methods of retrieving energy from trash. It is often said that the technology is there, waiting for the demand. We certainly have a need, but we must convince our communities of the feasibility. Knowledgeable presentation of the new ideas is essential to making changes.

22 Energy-Efficient Eating Habits

Materials:

- Fresh or preserved cut corn
- Fresh or preserved lima beans. (Many people prefer the taste of "baby" limas. Use any fresh or preserved shell beans such as lady peas or black-eyed peas.)

Background: Using locally grown vegetables from farms that practice organic gardening is a first, easy step in creating a diet that involves eating food that is not energy intensive to produce and transport. (Most chemical fertilizers are made from petroleum. They are certainly "organic" but are not the result of organic composting.)

There is a good, ecologically sound reason for eating more plant proteins and less animal proteins. Recall how much energy was lost by the time sun energy was passed to the carnivorous predator? By eating plant products, we are eating "closer to the sun." In other words, by using vegetable proteins for growth, more people can live on a portion of land than if they depend on meat raised on that land for protein. Many traditional combinations of grains are alternative protein sources. Rice and beans, corn and beans, or soy products are examples of complete proteins. These proteins are actually more usable by our bodies than is red meat. By contrast, it takes sixteen pounds of grain to create one pound of beef. That's a lot of lost energy between you and the sunshine. Also, cattle-grazing practices have created millions of acres of devastated native grassland. The whole country pays a very high cost for its beef habit.

Anytime we make a vegetable garden, we are recreating a field. By studying the relationships of plants and animals that live in meadows, we can learn to make better gardens.

Procedure: Make your own complete proteins out of plant products. Succotash is a native American dish that combines the incomplete proteins in corn and in beans to make a more complete, body-building protein. Long ago, indigenous people learned that diets of all corn or all beans were unhealthy, but if eaten in combination, the children grew stronger bodies and people lived with less disease. To make succotash, combine equal amounts of corn and beans and cook to your taste. (Less cooking not only uses less energy but will also give you more vitamins.)

Experiment with recipes from other cultures that have made similar discoveries. Look at corn tortillas and beans in Mexican cooking; rice and adzuki beans in Japanese cooking; tofu, tempeh, and soy sauce in many oriental dishes; and grain combinations in African-based cuisines such as Brazilian and Caribbean.

Trees and the Woods

WOODLOTS AND FORESTS

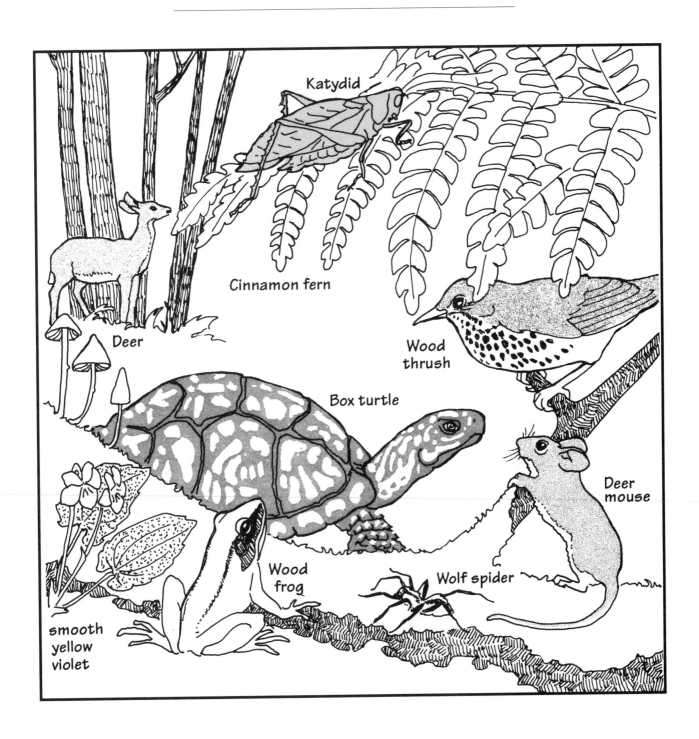

Katydid

Cinnamon fern

Deer

Wood thrush

Box turtle

Deer mouse

smooth yellow violet

Wood frog

Wolf spider

All by itself, a tree is a valuable example of how life systems operate. Its large and abundant parts can easily be studied to discover how the plants live, how they change with the seasons, and how other plants and animals depend on them. A large tree may create its own ecosystem, even altering its original habitat. Our oldest trees offer clues to our own history, and some show the results of our current environmental problems. As a renewable resource, trees are considered replaceable, but the fact is that some of the oldest forest ecosystems include plants and animals that cannot live in younger woodlands. These are currently threatened by logging practices that severely alter the habitat. Since many paper products are recyclable, there are numerous ways we can help save trees and woodlands, both in our neighborhoods and in distant forested lands.

Characteristics of the Area

Even if you have only one tree to observe, you will find evidence of the many topics discussed in this chapter. Your tree will change with the passing year, adding new growth or shedding some of its leaves, flowers, or seed structures. It will affect the

plants around it with its shade or dropped parts. It will be affected by winds, light, cold, and disease. Animals will use it for shelter or food. You may even find that you respond emotionally to the changes in your tree at the onset of autumn or the beginning of spring.

A group of trees, however, takes on aspects of the forest habitat, especially when their fallen leaves lie as a natural mulch, decaying and recycling their nutrients back into the soil. Once that simple cycle is in process, a host of other lives can be supported within the system. Small invertebrates such as insects and spiders can live there. The animals that eat these small invertebrates—mice, shrews, and birds—will follow. Larger predators will hunt for these smaller ones. Seedlings will sprout—those that live as companions to the trees and those that will eventually outgrow and overshadow their hosts. As the trees grow and change, they continue to change their environment. Weather and predators also act upon the standing trees, opening up some spots as others are filled in. The many-layered forest habitat is one of great diversity and wonderful complexity. Its organisms can be huge or tiny, year-round residents or tourists from the tropics.

In T.H. White's *The Once and Future King*, when the wizard Merlin wanted to expose the young Arthur to a source of ancient wisdom, he used his magic to slow down the movements of the forest trees so that Arthur could hear their language. You too will learn much about trees and woods by observing them carefully over long periods. Ecologists are just beginning to understand trees' subtlest "talk"—the chemical messages trees send to insects and even other trees. The study of the connections of roots and fungus threads that interlace the soil is also still in its early stages; we have only recently discovered that some individual soil fungi are the largest organisms on earth. Learning more about how the woodland ecosystem works is crucially important to people: Some of the endangered ecosystems may be irreplaceable, some may support life-saving medicinal plants, and some may be able to affect larger climate systems in ways still unknown.

The activities in this chapter can be used in the study of a single tree on several visits or during several seasons. Use the information you have learned from the one tree to investigate as many trees and woodlands as you can. Use the later activities to discover tree relationships as you explore the study site around the tree. After you study one forest area, try to explore other forests of different sizes, ages, and in different zones: wet, dry, northern, southern, mountain, and valley. The relationships and adaptations you find in each will illuminate the ecology of the others.

Common Inhabitants

The following plants and animals are commonly found in most of the woodland habitats of North America. If the area you study does not have all of these species, look for similar species and relationships that might be there.

PLANTS	ANIMALS
Woody trees and shrubs	Shrew
Oak	Woodfrog
Maple	Deer Mouse
Hornbeam	Red Eft
Pine	Vireo
Hemlock	Chickadee
Birch	Flying Squirrel
Huckleberry	Deer
	Bark Beetle
Herbaceous plants	Caterpillar
Fern	Katydid
Mushroom	Wolf Spider
Indian Pipe	Carpenter Ant
Beechdrop	Box Turtle
Violet	Thrush
	Ovenbird
	Tanager
	Woodpecker
	Gall Insect

Relationships to Look for

Indian pipe, fungi, and trees. Flowering stems of Indian pipe have a mysterious look about them; the stalks and flowers are white and waxy with pale pink tints to the inner blossoms. They appear only to bloom; the stiff clusters of several pipe-like flowering stems appearing suddenly under shady trees. They are able to exist without green leaves and photosynthesis or even extensive roots because of a special relationship with the trees around them. Their immediate source of water, sugar, and nutrients is the fibrous threads of mycellium (fungus) that enter at the base of their stems. But the mycellium gets most of its sugar from tree roots. The fungus exchanges soil nutrients and water for tree sugars. The Indian pipe has established itself as a third party in this system of exchanged resources to the point where it needs no roots or food-making mechanisms of its own. Its midsummer blossoms are evidence of mutual relationships that would otherwise be invisible to the passerby.

HOW TO FIND INDIAN PIPE

The growing plant is visible as a bent-over flower bud and a stem that stands about a hand's height when fully grown. The flower ripens and blooms with the stem still crooked, but as the seeds mature, the stem browns and straightens. This single gesture perhaps gives the plant its Latin name: *Monotropa* (single movement) *uniflora* (single flower). The brown pods full of tiny seeds stand alone or in small groups throughout the winter months. Your area may have plants that have evolved lifestyles similar to Indian pipe. Look for small, pale, leafless flowering stalks known as beech-drop, bear's breeches, or coralroot.

Bark beetles and dead wood. The wood-chewing larvae of various bark beetles play the very important role of opening dead wood to the recycling efforts of a host of decomposing organisms. Trees do excellent jobs of organizing particles into solid wood that resists decay. Standing deadwood represents stockpiles of nutrients and mineral elements that are available only when disassembled by the activities of fungi, molds, bacteria, and larger creatures, but the beetles usually make the first entries through the protective bark and into the cellulose fortress.

Female bark beetles lay eggs on dead wood at a site that suits the larvae's taste. The larvae hatch and eat their way through the wood; the larger beetles may make caverns into the safety of the inner heartwood. Usually pupating at the end of their tunnel, the winged adult chews its way to the surface and takes off to start a new generation.

HOW TO FIND BARK BEETLES

You can find adult beetles as they visit flowers for nectar and mate-finding. Many of the flower beetles with long antennae, the long-horned beetles, are bark beetles. For evidence of larvae, look under the loose section of dead wood bark or at the designs made by tunneling in the surface of bark-less wood. Individual tunnels show not just the length of the larva's work, but its increased girth and the pupal chamber. Look carefully for holes made by emerging adults. The irregular shape indicates the orientation of the beetle as it came out—the flatter side matches the flatter underpart of the beetle.

Tree twigs and oak twig pruners. Since healthy trees are able to fend off or limit the growth of would-be insect pests, successful tree-eating insects have usually evolved some method of circumventing a tree's defense tactics. A little beetle called an oak twig pruner prepares a twig by chewing off a circle of bark. Some sap goes into the tip, supporting life in the end section where the pruner lays her eggs. The twig stays alive long enough to feed the larvae during their early stages, but the damaged portion weakens the wood, and the twig is easily broken by a strong gust of wind. Carried to the ground, the larvae complete their growth inside the twig, safe from the tree's defense chemicals and in the more moderate ground-level climate.

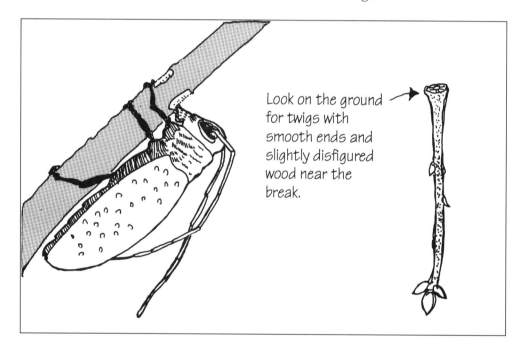

Look on the ground for twigs with smooth ends and slightly disfigured wood near the break.

HOW TO FIND TWIGS WITH TWIG PRUNERS

Beetle-pruned twigs can be found on the ground at any time of year, but freshly fallen ones can be seen from midsummer to fall. Squirrels will also create pruned twig litter by biting off twigs to get at sap or to reach galls at the tips of the buds. A beetle-pruned twig is identifiable by a slightly swollen base and a smooth-looking cut where the larvae have continued eating through the wood. A squirrel's cut will look as though it was snipped by sharp shears. Oak trees are frequently used by the beetles, but also check under maples, poplars, locusts, and fruit and nut trees.

The Life Processes of a Tree

Although most trees grow in a similar way, each individual tree is continually responding to its particular environment—a balsam spruce on a windy mountaintop looks very different from a balsam spruce in a sheltered valley. You can learn to interpret environmental conditions by learning about the ways trees grow.

1 How a Branch Grows

Materials:

- The growing tip of any woody branch

Background: A tree attains its shape by expanding slowly outward. Our bodies grow by enlarging every part, but a branch grows longer at its tip ends, where the buds have formed. Every nonflower bud will grow into a section of twig and new leaves. At the same time that the buds open and grow, the tree adds a layer of woody tissue just under the bark of the trunk and branches. The tree is alive only in the thin, new layers just under the bark; the past years' inner deadwood provides support and plumbing.

Procedure: Look for the growth rings that mark off the yearly growth sections along a branch. You will see indentations encircling the twig like bracelets. Count back along the stem as many years as you can distinguish. (The buildup of bark will eventually cover the rings.) Why might some year's growth be less than that of others?

By the end of every growing season, most woody plants have formed buds or bud clusters at the tips of their twigs. Since the next year's growth begins at the bud site, the scars formed by bud scales can be used to count the age of the twig.

123

2 **Finding the Living Tissues of a Tree**

Materials:

- A piece of wood showing a cross section of growth rings (firewood or lumber scraps are good possibilities)
- Salad oil
- Saw for smoothing a piece (optional)

Background: The living tissues of the tree's insides are mainly a kind of plumbing system. The cellulose tubes that bring water and nutrients into the tree are called xylem. They work only in one direction: up. Each xylem tube carries a thin thread of water from the soil to a leaf. Another system of transport cells carries the sugar and nutrients from the leaves to growth sites throughout the tree. Instead of strong tubes, the phloem cells form a spongy strata of thin, squishy cells. These soft cells only last a year. Made new each spring, the phloem tissue lives between the most recent layer of xylem and the most recent inner layer of protective bark cells.

Phloem and xylem cells are both created out of the remarkable layer of cells that lie between them called the cambium.

It is the cambium that responds to wounds, to seasonal changes, and to the effects of light or shade. Almost invisible itself, the cambium makes the tree the shape you see. Covering every living twig and branch, in a sense, this ghosty, glove-like layer is really the living tree.

Procedure: Find a cross section of a tree's trunk or large branch. A piece of firewood or scrap lumber will do. Make a fresh saw cut if the end is too rough or rotten. To enhance the contrast of the parts, brush the smooth section of the wood with cooking oil. Count the yearly rings, noticing differences in growth. Try to find the parts described above.

Any board end has annual rings made by xylem cells. The spring xylem cells are larger than those made in late summer. Summer wood is usually denser and darker. Count both spring and summer layers as one year's growth.

3 How Roots Grow

Materials:

- Radish seeds
- Sponge or paper towel
- Clear plastic bag (bread bag)

Background: Like the extending tips of woody twigs, the roots of trees and shrubs also grow outward. The tips of surface roots extend approximately to the place in the soil where rain drips off the leaves at the end of the longest lower branches. The newest growth on a root tip are white and delicate hairs, each a single cell. As the root tip tunnels through the soil, new arrays of hair grow just behind the tip and then die and are shed as the root works its way through new soil particles.

Each particle is surrounded by a water film containing dissolved mineral nutrients such as nitrogen and phosphorus. As the root hair comes in contact with this solution, the nutrient "soup" moves through the root hair's membrane. The membrane lets in only the particular nutrients the plant needs, and once the water is inside, the root can exert some pressure to start the water up to the leaves.

Procedure: Sprouting radish seeds have root hairs that are similar to those of woody plants. You can easily see the hairs if you grow some radish, turnip, or cabbage seeds on a wet sponge or a dampened paper towel. Put the seeds and sponge in a plastic bag. In a day or so, you can see the fuzzy white root hairs emerging just behind the growing root tip. Find out how long individual root hairs live by marking a few new hairs with marker ink, then observing the sequence of root growth and the formation of new hairs. How long does one hair live? If you can turn the sprouting setup in different directions every few days, watch how the root "knows where down is" no matter which way the sponge is turned.

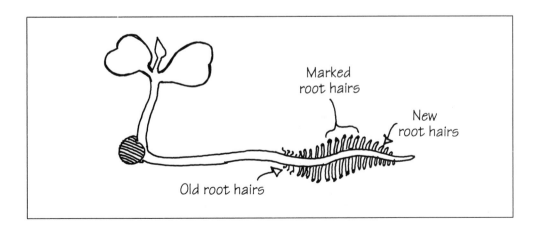

Marked root hairs

New root hairs

Old root hairs

4 How Water Moves Through a Tree

Materials:

- Leaves on a tree that you can easily reach (broad leaves work better than evergreens)
- At least two plastic bags

Background: Once water enters the tree by its roots, it forms a slender strand of water and nutrients that extends unbroken through the xylem from root tip to an opening in the bark or a leaf. As a little of the strand evaporates from the opening, more fluid is pulled from below like a rope hauled in hand over hand. Wind, heat, and sunlight increase evaporation and, therefore, the movement of water through the tree. Since every tree has millions of openings, a tree in effect is a living fountain, spouting invisible water vapor from every pore. The new xylem cells that form the wood of the tree cover last year's wood as a layer of fine, thin tubes. The tubes are made of stacks of a kind of cell that is strong on four sides but so thin at its top and bottom that a strand of stacked cells can act as a straw to pull water from the ground.

Transpiration is the evaporation of water from the plant. As water vapor leaves the plant through a breathing pore, or stomata, more water enters the plant. This transport pathway of water and dissolved nutrients can be traced through the cell wall of a root hair (1), along the root (2), and throughout the plant to various stoma (3).

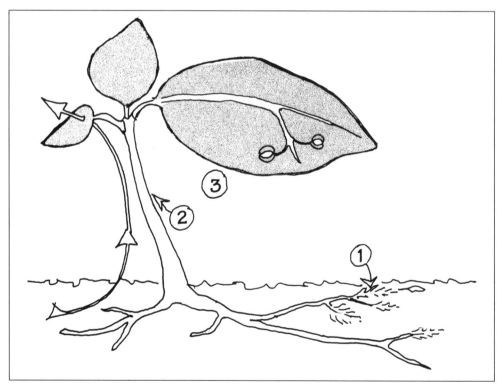

Procedure: If you contain water vapor as it evaporates from the leaves, it will condense as droplets of water that you can see or even measure. To see the effect of sunshine on the rate of water loss, set up two experiments. Tie one plastic bag so that it fits over a few leaves that are in direct sunshine. Tie another over the same number of shaded leaves on the same tree. After an hour (or perhaps longer) inspect each bag for water droplets. Which set of leaves produced the most moisture? You might want to repeat the experiment (with dry bags) overnight and compare the results.

Like a map of city streets, the veins of a leaf show the transport system of water and nutrients.

A Tree's Life History

5 What Happens When a Tree Dies?

Materials:

- A piece of rotting wood
- Plastic bag or sheet to contain the pieces and keep the wood moist
- Glass jars and magnifying glass for observing any animals
- Optional—piece of dry, fresh wood for contrast

Background: A tree is made of water and mineral nutrients woven in delicate and resilient patterns by the cambium, the inner, living layer of wood just behind the bark. A tree's body is cellulose and it runs on sugar, which it makes itself with only the sunlight for power. Now, imagine that a tree is dying—its components are breaking down and returning to the earth. Once the cambium's life energy is extinguished, the tree's power to defend itself is gone, and the energy and nutrients that are locked in the cellulose molecules are sought by bacteria, mold, fungi, and beetles. Branch by branch or all at once, the tree falls and becomes part of the soil. Fungi and soil creatures digest the wood, unlocking the molecules to feed their own bodies.

As you observe the breakdown of rotting wood back to soil, imagine a tree cut as firewood and burned. As the energy stored in the cellulose is released as flames, it is as though the sunlight the tree had absorbed were being released. When the fire is out and the heat, light, and steam are gone, all that remains are the minerals: a pile of soft, grey ashes. These are the essential, skeletal elements that once helped give structure to the tree. As mineral nutrients, they can mix with rainwater, enter the roots of another tree, and be built into wood again.

Procedure: Find a rotting piece of wood and carefully take it apart. If you have a piece of firm wood handy, you can compare the differences in texture, firmness, moisture, and smell. Look for delicate white or yellow branching threads of fungi (called hyphae) growing throughout the rotten wood. As fungi and the millions of invisible bacteria digest the cellulose, they soften the structure and make the wood available to a variety of larger creatures such as worms, bark beetles, millipedes, and sowbugs. As long as the wood stays moist, the breakdown will continue. Be sure to return the wood and any creatures you discovered to the place you found the wood.

6 Comparing Trees

Materials:

- Several deciduous trees of the same species

Background: It is very rare to find two trees exactly alike. Each individual has its own rhythm of branching, time of leafing, and a recognizable individuality to the shape of its leaves.

Procedure: As you study the growth patterns and cycles of a particular tree, find another tree of the same species and compare their shapes and textures. Look at the texture of the bark, the way the twigs branch, and the shapes of buds and leaves. Look for similarities as well as differences. Keep in mind that some same-species trees in groups are actually sprouts off the roots of one original plant. Clusters of poplars, aspens, locust trees, sassafras, tupelos, and American beeches are probably all root sprouts of just one "parent" plant.

Make a collection of leaves from three or four different broad-leaved (deciduous) trees. Sort them according to habitat differences such as exposure to sunlight or dryness of soil. Can you spot any influences of habitat?

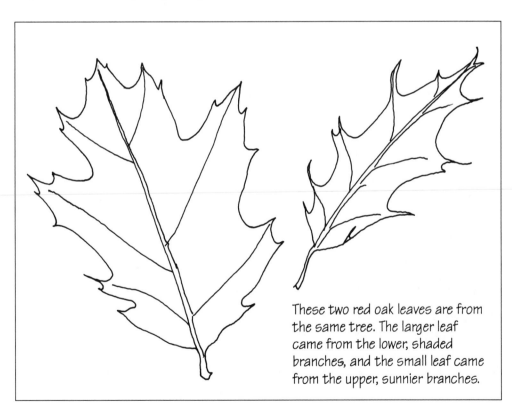

These two red oak leaves are from the same tree. The larger leaf came from the lower, shaded branches, and the small leaf came from the upper, sunnier branches.

Trees and the Seasons

As the largest plants, trees often provide the background and definition of our sense of seasonal change. A knowledge of the ways that nearby trees respond to the seasons can bring us to a better understanding of our responses to the seasons' wheel of changes.

7 | Forcing Spring Buds in Winter

Materials:

- Length of branch that includes several buds
- Clippers to make a clean branch cut

Background: The leafless tree branches of winter seem dead and lifeless, but any branch with buds is simply waiting for warmth to bring life to the leaves and stems within the buds. Many twigs can be tricked into a spring response.

Procedure: Northern trees, especially, need several weeks of freezing weather to reset their "ready-to-bud" mechanisms. Without that inhibition, they might start leafing out during a December warm spell and lose all their leaves for next year. After the winter solstice, about the end of January, cut and bring into your home a forearm's length of a leafless, deciduous tree branch. Put the branch in water, as you would cut flowers, and observe the opening events. The first events will be invisible—the starch and sugars stored in the branch will convert to a form the cells can use for growth. Growth will begin with the enlarging of the bud scales (on those buds that have protective scales). As the scales fall away, you will see the new leaves and stems, already formed, begin to expand and extend toward the light. Look for flowers, as well. They may be cone-like catkins or clusters of small flowers. Many tree species have separate male and female flowers, in some species on separate trees.

Looking at Tree Flowers

Many trees have very light pollen that is moved about by the wind. These trees have small numerous blossoms located at the top and branch tips of the tree. (You may find some blooming tips on the ground, discarded by a squirrel who has bitten off the outer twigs to get at the flow of sweet sap.)

Look carefully along a tree's twig tips in fall, winter, or early spring. If you see light green or pale red cone-like structures, you know that the tree uses wind to pollinate its flowers. Whether the flowers resemble braided fingers or squat cones, wind pollinated flowers are called catkins. Watch to see if the pollen-bearing male catkins bloom at the same time as the female or seed-making catkins on the same tree. (Some species have all male or all female trees.)

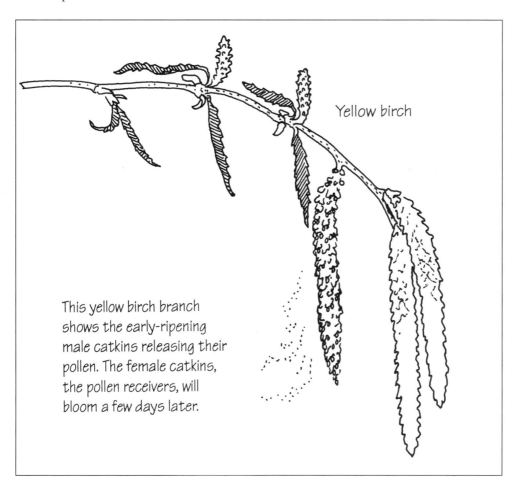

Yellow birch

This yellow birch branch shows the early-ripening male catkins releasing their pollen. The female catkins, the pollen receivers, will bloom a few days later.

8 Flowering Pines and Flying Pine Seeds

Materials:

- Cones from a pine, spruce, fir, or hemlock
- Water

Background: You may already be aware of the flowering of local cone-bearing evergreens. In late spring, you might have seen the pale yellow dust layering a car windshield or collecting on the edge of a pond or puddle. Shortly after the pollen falls, the source of the pollen, the male catkins, are dropped from the trees. They litter the ground like pale, pinkish caterpillars. The female catkins, the woody cones, are still on the tree. The seeds that have been fertilized by the windblown pollen grains will grow just under the cone scales, perhaps for several years, before they are released to the wind in their turn.

Left to right:
digger pine, white pine, pinyon, pitch pine, loblolly pine, sugar pine.

The seeds will have the best chance to grow well if they are blown to a sunny field, away from the shaded soil beneath the parent trees. Most cones have a built-in mechanism that releases the seeds only in dry (and perhaps windy) weather. When wet, the cone stays closed, reducing the chance that the seeds will fall with the rain to the soil beneath the parent tree.

Procedure: You can test this response in any evergreen seed cone that has become ripe and able to open. Some cones may not be ripe enough and other species, such as pitch pine and jack pine, may open their scales only in response to the heat of a fire. Any cast-off cones that you find on the ground will work. Experiment with your cone's responses to rain by wetting one and watching what it does. Also try drying a wet cone. If you have two cones, keep one unchanged to compare it with the one you alter. If your cones still have seeds in them, experiment to see under which conditions the most seeds are released.

9 Finding Tree Seeds

Materials:

- Writing materials
- A copy of the sample chart or one with a similar format

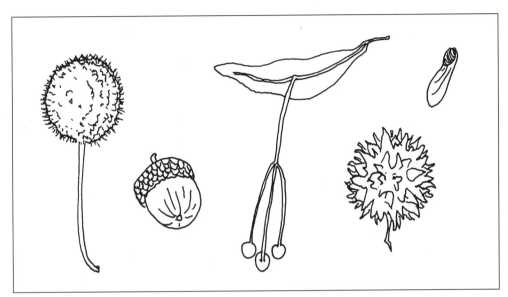

Examples of Tree Seeds: *Left to right:* sycamore, red oak, basswood, sweet gum, white pine.

Background: Each species of tree has its own means of getting its seeds away from the area that the individual "parent" tree already is using. Some trees (cherries, apples, dogwoods) may produce sweet or attractive fruit around the seeds, which are eaten by birds and "planted" elsewhere when the birds defecate. Some trees (maples, ashes, sycamores, pines, and poplars) have seeds with attachments like propellers or feathery fluff; these seeds are transported by the wind.

Some trees (oaks, beeches, hickories) have large seeds with lots of meat inside them. These round seeds can roll a short distance but they can be carried off greater distances by animals. Squirrels, for instance, are very good at burying seeds, some of which sprout if left uneaten. Jays and nutcrackers are the best tree planters of all; they will travel miles to and from nut-bearing trees and hide the seeds in their territories for later consumption. Since they prefer to nest in piney, old field habitats, they can be the main agents in turning pine woods into mixed hardwood forests through the sprouting of forgotten nuts.

Procedure: If you have found flowers on the trees in your locale, you can keep track of when their seeds ripen and how their seeds are dispersed. Keep track of the seed-ripening dates of several trees. On the appropriate days, try to observe where ripe seeds travel and end up.

10 Nut Collecting

Materials:

- A quantity of nuts or other tree seeds (grocery stores have bags of peanuts and hard shelled nuts if you can't find any outdoors)

Background: Most nut trees produce large quantities of seeds at one time. Perhaps the tree's strategy is to flood the market with enough food that numbers of nut-eaters will be attracted and take the surplus seeds back to their territories to be stashed away. If forgotten, the cached nuts might sprout and grow.

Procedure: Collect a quantity of nuts in the late summer and fall. Compare textures, sizes, firmness, and smell of a variety of species. Sort them into categories—those likely to be eaten by birds, those likely to be blown by wind, and those likely to be carried away by animals. See if you can find evidence of these processes in your locale—i.e., a grove of maples or a succession of oaks. Save some nuts for a week or more and see if any changes occur. You may see signs of ripening or evidence that the nuts provide food and shelter for tiny creatures. Nut-eating insects such as beetles and weevils may emerge, and the seed husks may open.

11 Sprouting Found Nuts

Materials:

- Several freshly collected nuts or tree seeds
- Soil and pots (any waterproof containers such as milk cartons can be used. Make holes in the bottom for drainage)

Background: A nut is made up of a shell, a packet or two of stored food, and a tiny tree. Although the tree is still embryonic, it is sensitive to the conditions surrounding it and will start to grow only when specific conditions of temperature, moisture, light, or even decay are sensed. By being fussy, the potential tree is more likely to sprout when its particular needs will be met by its environment.

Procedure: Try sprouting some nuts or seeds by keeping them moist, then grow them in pots or in a garden outside. Some kinds of nuts are inhibited from sprouting right away by a chemical programming *not* to sprout until they have gone through a winter or even two. (Horticultural guides can tell you which ones. Look under "stratifying seeds.") Apple seeds are examples of seeds that require stratifying. You can sometimes hurry the process along by using your freezer to put your apple seeds through a 2-month "winter" and then try to grow them in soil in pots or outside.

12 Understanding Color Changes in Leaves

Materials:

- A collection of freshly fallen autumn leaves

Background: Why do you think some trees lose their leaves before winter comes? As much as trees need leaves to make their food, broad leaves in winter would catch snow and break large limbs, thus most trees need to get rid of some or all of their leaves before winter comes. Slimmed down to just buds and branches, a deciduous tree is more likely to survive the weight of ice and snow. (Even evergreens lose some leaves in fall, usually shedding all their two-year-old needles.) Before the leaves fall to the ground, however, they usually turn shades of yellow, orange, and red, making autumn a very beautiful time of year.

Procedure: Make a collection of fresh autumn leaves. Using the following information, look for examples of the various ways leaves turn color in the fall.

The green summer colors last longest along the mid-rib and veins. We see the fall colors only after the green chlorophyll breaks down. The edges of the leaf dry first, and the chlorophyll remains in the parts of the leaf where the water still stands in the central tubes. As the days shorten the chlorophyll breaks down and the leaf stem grows a dense layer of cells where the leaf attaches to the twig. This brittle cork layer allows the leaf to break cleanly off the tree.

The red and purply colors form only where sunlight hits the leaf directly. Shaded or partially shaded leaves will be yellow in any area out of direct sunlight. (You can see this phenomenon on red apples at any time of year. The reddest side of any apple is that which faced the sun. You might notice yellow "photos" of stems or leaves in places where the apple skin was shaded.) A series of cloudy days in fall will produce yellower rather than redder leaves.

Trees as Homes for Other Organisms

Once a young tree begins to make leaves and wood, it begins to create new "real estate." A tree is like a continent that contains many habitats for other organisms. The varying conditions of temperature, exposure, dryness, and moisture make diverse microhabitats all over the tree.

13 Looking for Plants That Live on Trees

Materials:

- Writing materials (paper, pencil)
- Ruler

Background: Look over the surface of a tree's bark and branches for other plants making themselves at home. Small seedlings of other trees may have managed to sprout in the moisture of a crevice, lichens or mosses may be encrusting the bark, or coarse epiphytes such as Spanish moss may be growing harmlessly on a high perch. What you find will depend on where you live and the conditions surrounding your tree.

You may find some plants that are parasitic on a tree's resources. In many Southern states, mistletoe clusters can be seen in winter as evergreen spheres high on the branches of deciduous trees. Mistletoe supplements the food made by its own green leaves by sending shallow roots into the sugar flow of its host. Although the sticky white berries are poisonous to people, birds seek them out as food. After feeding, some berries may adhere to the bird's bill and in the act of wiping its bill on a branch, the bird innocently plants new mistletoe.

Any parasite plays a risky game: Dependent on the resources of the host, it cannot live so as to endanger the host's existence while it still needs the host's resources. In the sense that all organisms are dependent on particular "host" ecosystems for their existence, this is a "courtesy" that makes the rule in nature. Human disasters such as severe erosion, poisoned soil, and crop loss due to acid rain are examples of overdrawing on the environmental account, creating a resource deficit, and endangering our own existence.

Lichens

The relationship of plants that create the lichens shows us a balanced and beneficent parasitism (see page 162). A variety of lichens may be living on the surface of tree trunks and limbs. Lichens are very sensitive to moisture and grow more densely clustered on a surface that is both moist and sunny. In habitats where sunny surfaces are drier, lichens have to make do with the shady, usually north-facing surface. Look for clusters near the base of the tree or on lower branches where rainwater trickling down the tree makes a more nutrient rich and moister habitat. Lichens are good indicators of air quality; they are absent or sparse where exposed to car exhaust or industrial air pollution.

Procedure: Once you begin to observe the lichens in your area, you'll probably find that only a few kinds live on trees. Notice differences such as color, texture, and general shape to distinguish each lichen. Go on a lichen hunt. Write down at least four sites on trees where each type of lichen is found. Identify the tree species if possible and measure the largest lichen at each site. Write down a description of each lichen's best habitat, based on your recorded information.

14 Finding Insects That Live Inside Leaves

Materials:

- Plants with galls
- Magnifying glass
- A book with information on gall insect identification

Background: In the spring, tiny gall-making insects lay eggs in new leaves. The young then burrow into the leaf, eating the tissue and secreting a chemical that replicates the plant's own growth hormone. This causes the leaf to form extra spongy cells. The insect completes its growth within the gall and emerges as a winged adult. (Although the gall itself is probably not debilitating to a tree, a plant stressed by drought or pollution is likely to have more galls than will a healthy tree.) Perhaps the healthy tree resembles a healthy ecosystem—an unstressed tree is able to maintain a variety of complex chemicals which help it maintain a balanced relationship in its environment. An intact ecosystem has a similar healthy complexity and resistance to disease.

Procedure: Look for strangely shaped, somewhat symmetrical lumps on some of the leaves and stems; some will be galls, the homes for young aphids, wasps, or flies. You may be curious to open a gall. Inside, you are likely to find a single grub (larva wasp or fly) or a colony of aphids or tiny mites. Please limit your investigations—opening a gall destroys the home of the helpless inhabitants.

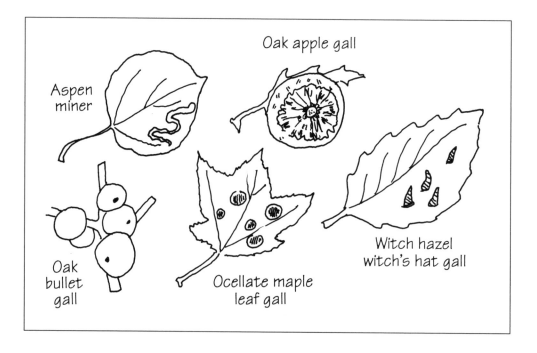

Oak apple gall

Aspen miner

Oak bullet gall

Ocellate maple leaf gall

Witch hazel witch's hat gall

15 Caterpillars and Trees

Materials:

- A container for observing caterpillars

  Note: Some fuzzy caterpillars have brittle hairs that can cause rashes on tender skin. Never blow into a container with a fuzzy caterpillar inside—loose hairs may embed in your eye!

Background: Caterpillars are major predators on forest trees. For the caterpillars, a tree full of leaves is a perfect situation: all the food they can eat and all in the species most desired, a choice usually made by the female moths who lay their eggs on the branches or leaves. In a balanced ecosystem, natural predators such as beetles, tree bugs, parasitic wasps, and birds crop the caterpillar populations so that their leaf-eating doesn't greatly endanger the tree's overall sugar production.

An easy way to find out what moths are living in your area is to leave an incandescent outdoor light on during the night and check for moths in the morning. A moth identification book may also tell you what trees each species eats as a caterpillar.

Occasionally, however, the caterpillars get the upper hand, consuming a large enough proportion of a tree's leaves to alter the tree's usual ecology. Passive though the trees may seem, they have evolved chemical responses that are very effective against infestations. The trees produce chemicals called phenols, which flavor the leaves (the bitter tannin of tea and oak leaves is a phenol) and make the leaves more difficult to digest. The caterpillars grow more slowly and may even fail to reach their final metamorphosis—the moth stage. At the very least these smaller caterpillars become smaller moths and lay fewer eggs than normal. The trees are also able to add phenols to just *some* leaves, causing the caterpillars to search out the more edible leaves. The extra movement not only means that the caterpillars will take longer to feed themselves into pupahood but are more likely to be picked off by watchful birds. Research shows that not only the threatened tree develops protective phenols, but nearby trees respond to airborne chemicals released by the damaged leaves by increasing the phenol content of their own leaves.

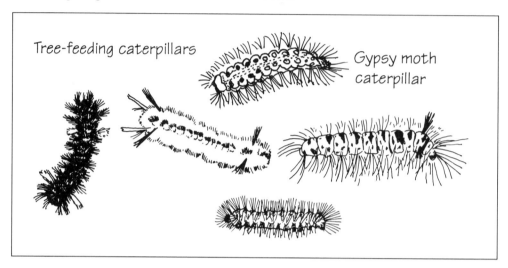

Tree-feeding caterpillars

Gypsy moth caterpillar

Procedure: Search for clues of caterpillars on trees. Caterpillars eat larger chunks of leaves than do most other insects. Search for eaten, rolled, or folded leaves, little brown droppings on the ground under branches, or thick webs at the bases of the branches (tent caterpillars) or at their tips (fall webworm). Once you start looking for damaged leaves you will start to find caterpillars everywhere. Finding an *uneaten* leaf may actually be more of a challenge.

Gypsy Moths and Oak Trees

An interesting insight into the complexity of the interrelationships between caterpillars and trees has emerged from the studies done on gypsy moths and oak trees. Gypsy moths were introduced into this country by accident, escapees from an attempt to cultivate caterpillars for silk thread production. With no natural predators, gypsy moth populations exploded into the forests, stripping acres of leaves before the caterpillars turned into moths. In the one hundred years since their first appearance, some native birds have learned to eat them, various poisons have been tried, and nonnative insect predators have also been introduced. Unfortunately, the last two methods have also decimated native caterpillars, as well. The most effective procedure for controlling the species seems to be to let the population build until a disease virus is able to develop in the crowded population. If attempts are made to continually reduce the population, the caterpillars stay scattered and the virus cannot develop. It has been found, however, that as the numbers rise and the leaves are stripped, the oak trees begin producing tannin, which, instead of acting as a further limit to predation, seems to *help* the caterpillars by acting as an anti-viral medication. Gypsy moth caterpillars feeding on trees with high concentrations of phenols are less likely to get the virus (although they do lay fewer eggs). On trees that produce less phenols, such as aspens, the caterpillars readily catch the virus and die off.

Even when their natural protective chemicals seem to fail, as in the oak-and-gypsy-moth study, trees have a backup system against defoliation. The trees may seem completely stripped, but their backup leaf buds can unfurl a new set of leaves late in the summer. The oak woods look like spring again, long after the gypsy moths have emerged, mated, and deposited eggs for next year. Although the damage may be extensive, the deciduous trees can recover unless large caterpillar populations continue for several years. In fact, recovery may be slower in areas where gypsy moth poisons are sprayed. Observers in untended oak woodlands report that succeeding summers bring good growth and recovery since the caterpillar droppings fertilize the tree roots better than do the rot-resistant oak leaves.

16 Captive Caterpillars

Materials:

- Caterpillar
- Leaves from the plant on which it was found
- Container with air holes

Background: If you find a caterpillar, notice where it lives and return each day to observe its progress and changes. If you can keep it supplied with fresh leaves from the tree species on which you found it, consider taking it home for closer observation on its feeding habits and life cycle.

Procedure: *Note:* Do not collect any caterpillar unless you are able to tend to its daily needs of fresh leaves and frass (excrement) removal. A caterpillar's life is dangerous enough without the added threat of careless collectors.

If you can easily tend to their needs, caterpillars provide a fascinating study of growth and change. Use the following guidelines to improve your chances of successful care.

- In its initial stages, a caterpillar won't need a container if it is on a branch with lots of fresh leaves that it likes. Keep the branch or twigs in fresh water, using a small-mouthed jar with a cotton plug at the opening to keep the caterpillar from climbing down the branch into the water. Caterpillars produce lots of droppings, so a paper-lined tray under the setup is helpful.

Annie is experimenting to find out which kind of tree leaves Japanese beetles will eat.

- When the caterpillar reaches its maximum size, it will stop eating and start wandering. Even if you can provide the perfect conditions for pupation (either a stick support or loose soil, depending on the species), the caterpillar may need to move about for a set time. It will need containment at this stage—a butterfly emerging in your house in winter from a hidden chrysalis is very disappointing.

- Once the caterpillar has changed into a pupa, it is dependent on outdoor conditions to time its emergence. If its container is safe from hungry mice and has support and room for the emerging wings, put the setup outside where conditions are moderate and accurate for the season. Bring it back inside in the spring so you can watch for the "coming out" event. (Caterpillars are parasitized fairly often. A parasitic wasp may emerge instead of a butterfly or moth. They are harmless to people and important members of the local ecosystem. Let it go as you would the butterfly.)

- Knowing which species you have will help you figure when to expect it to emerge from its pupa. Although some moths and butterflies do complete their growth cycle in early summer, most late-summer caterpillars will pupate all winter; others will emerge in fall to lay eggs and die. You will find that not many books identify caterpillars by their species, but look in libraries and bookstores for good illustrations.

17 Birds of the Woods Report

Background: When you notice a bird moving quietly about in a tree, it is probably looking for caterpillars or other insects to eat. Each bird has a distinctive style of hunting as well as dispatching its prey. If it is early summer, you may be able to find the bird's nest by noticing where it takes the food it has found. Many of the insect-eating birds of the forest are small, leaf-sized, and able to make quick, darting movements. Warblers, vireos, kinglets, chickadees, and gnatcatchers are the smaller of the treetop tribe. If they are moving along the trunk and limbs, they may be nuthatches, woodpeckers, black and white warblers, or brown creepers. Look among the leaves on the woodland floor for foragers such as thrushes, robins, or ovenbirds.

The various woodland bird species may be using different parts of the tree as their territory. A gnatcatcher, for example, hunting in a high crotch near the top of the tree, may never cross paths with the ovenbird that hunts on the ground.

Procedure: What are the birds doing in your trees? Be a reporter of ornithological events, snooping for news of the feathered and famous. When you spot a bird, watch it carefully and try to figure out what it is doing. If the bird is feeding, what techniques is it using to find food? What problems is it dealing with? In what ways is it using its environment to meet its needs for food and shelter? In what ways is it affecting or changing other organisms? Try to see the area through the eyes of the bird, but be careful not to give the bird human thoughts or concerns. Follow the golden rule of all news reporters as you record your observations: Your facts must stand up to the question, How do you know? Include the following in your report:

- Where the bird is located (place, time, weather)
- Its identity or significant colors or markings
- What is it doing? Include the ideas mentioned above
- A drawing showing the bird in its environment

Reporter's Notes:

Where: _____

_____

Who: _____

_____

Observed behavior:_____

_____

Include a sketch of how the bird fits into its environment.

18 Old Trees As Homesites

Materials:

- Writing materials for list making
- Optional art materials to illustrate the relationships of trees and animals

Background: Even when it is dead, a tree is important to the ecosystem. Look on standing dead trees for the neat circular or oval holes that woodpeckers make. These are entrance holes to nesting cavities that have been hollowed out of the center of the tree. Feeding sites, where woodpeckers have been chiseling at wood in the search for beetles, will have hole that are ragged and irregular instead of round or oval.

Once the young woodpeckers have abandoned their home, the cavities become crucial for the survival of smaller winter birds. On cold winter nights, chickadees and titmice will flock into woodpecker cavities to spend the long, dark hours in warm and crowded safety.

Standing dead trees are important to the lives of many animals. Owls, raccoons, deer mice, flying squirrels, and grey squirrels often take over and enlarge old woodpecker cavities. In small tunnels of their own making, beetle larva, termites, and carpenter ants may also reside. The lives connect and interweave in patterns that include predators and prey of deadwood inhabitants. All organisms considered, a standing deadwood snag represents one of the cornerstones of the woodland ecosystem.

Procedure: List all the creatures in your area that might live in a snag such as this; then make a list of all the animals that eat them or are eaten by them (including plants). You might make a chart or mural showing where in the snag each animal might live and include a sketch of its food if it is found outside of the tree.

Standing deadwood snag

19 Time Traveling: Looking for Clues of Past and Future Events

Materials:

- Paper and pen or pencil

Background: The look of the woodland is always changing. Young forests may be found in a neglected field, and an old woodland may have remnants of fences or walls where there used to be pasture. If the young trees in the woods are a different species from the older ones (for instance, pines under oaks), you can imagine the effects over the next fifty years: Will the woods be darker? Will young pines overtake the oaks?

Procedure: Look for some of the following clues to past and future events:

- Big trees with large lower limbs. The lower limbs may be dead if the tree is surrounded by younger trees. (Large trees, especially nut trees, were commonly left to grow in a pasture to provide shade and treats for animals and farmers.)

- Hillsides that become unexpectedly flattened, perhaps leveled for farming.

- Many hardwood trees with several trunks coming from one root system, an indication of regrowth from stumps after logging. (Most conifers cannot send up sprouts when cut down.)

- Thick grapevines in the woods. The young vines began growing when the trees were saplings in a sunny field and kept growing as the trees rose.

Double-trunk tree

As you explore your area, list any clues you find to past events or hints of habitats to come.

20 Finding a Home in the Woods

Materials:

- Writing materials
- A copy of the questions in this activity

Procedure: Pretend to be a small furry creature who is looking for a home in the woods. (Choose an animal you have observed or make up one adapted to life in a woodland.) Your home must provide you with shelter and be near some source of food. You will need water, too—how much depends on your size. (Deer need a brook or pond, mice can do with dew.) Take into consideration seasonal changes in deciding how much territory you will need. Decide whether your home can also support the needs of a mate and offspring. (You might find a place first and then make up an imaginary creature to fit the habitat.) Record the following survival stipulations:

- Will you eat meat, seeds, or leaves? Where can they be found in your habitat? What physical parts or adaptive behaviors do you have that will help you keep nourished, even when the season changes?

- What other plants and animals are important to your survival? Are they found in the woods? Do other animals influence the plants you need for shelter or food? Do other animals compete with you for the things you need?

- How will you escape predation? At what point in your life cycle are you the most vulnerable? What adaptations will help you survive?

- How will you find a mate? (Signaling for a mate without alerting a predator is always a problem for animals. Consider the use of scents, color changes, sounds, or markings in the environment.)

- Describe the pathway of energy from sunshine to plants to you. What natural events would threaten your energy strand? What human activities might cause problems?

Woodland Mushrooms: Essential Participants

Mushroom plants seem to grow magically during the summer months. Overnight, an individual or a cluster will appear on a dead tree or the ground. Fibrous threads, called hyphae, produce the mushroom when the plant is ready to make reproducive spores. Although they are principally agents of decay, soil fungi are able to snare and consume microscopic creatures. They can also extract sugars from tree roots in trade for freshly digested soil nutrients.

The underground threads of the mushroom plant run throughout the soil, transporting nutrients, decomposing dead leaves and animals, and even preying upon soil organisms.

21   Mycorrhizae: The Partnership of Fungi and Trees

Materials:

- Fresh amounts of decaying leaves (at least a year on the ground) or a piece of rotting wood, soft enough to crumble in your hands.

Background: The above-ground mushroom is only the "fruit" of the rest of the plant. The fungus that makes the mushroom is a loosely organized system of delicate strands. The strands spread throughout moist soil, growing densely wherever moist organic material is found. Once sufficient energy is available and underground reproduction has occurred, the spore-making "toadstool" appears.

Procedure: Pull apart some well-rotted leaves or wood until you find delicate white or orangish mushroom threads, called **hyphae,** growing throughout the rotted material. These are the spongy strands of the mushroom plant that grow throughout moist soil, absorbing nutrients from dead organic material.

Some fungi enter living tree roots from which they absorb tree sugars made by the leaves high above. The trees also benefit from this alliance by absorbing nutrients directly through the hyphae, called **mycorrhizae** in their new function. Since plant roots must otherwise absorb only through constantly growing root tips, these more permanent channels of water and nutrients give the plant a better chance at survival. The roots of some common woodland plants show swellings where the fungus enters. Without harming any rare species, check the roots of the most common plants in your woodland. Bracken ferns are a good choice if they are abundant.

The northern flying squirrel eats underground mushrooms (truffles). The spores are concentrated, mixed with yeast and nutrients, then excreted by the squirrel. Once in the soil, the spores grow into hyphae that become mycorrhizae on the roots of woody plants, perhaps benefiting the trees that feed the flying squirrels.

Life in the Woodland Soil

Once soil ecologists began to investigate the connections between fungi and green plants, the notion of single trees competing for sunlight by outgrowing competitors gave way to a much more complex image. Not only does a single oak or pine share resources with soil fungi, they also share with each other and with other smaller plants around them. Young maple trees growing near each other become linked together as the roots grow into each other and fuse to form a single system. In effect, the taller trees become the higher branches for the younger ones by sharing their sugars with them. The root system of the younger contributes to the larger system by absorbing surface water and nutrients. A number of pine seedlings were observed as they grew together over a fifteen-year period. After ten years, all their roots had grown together, and although one tree was cut down, its stump continued to add growth rings as though it were a living branch stub.

22 Investigating Soils

Materials:

- Trowel and paper for displaying material found. (In soft woodland soils, a bare hand might be sufficient.)

Background: Soils will vary according to the plants that grow in that environment, how the land has been used, and the local climate. The thickness of the leaf litter, for instance, is strongly influenced by the chemical makeup of the leaves of nearby plants. Leaves of trees that are lower in acid and phenol, such as aspens, maples, and birches, break down more rapidly than the tannin-laden leaves of oaks, pines, and beeches. If you examine the soil in areas where there are long, cold winters, the litter will be thicker than in the warmer South where the soil bacteria, fungi, and earthworms have more time to break down the leaves to nutrients. Even a simple investigation such as digging with your hand or with a trowel can give you an idea of what soil is made of and how different kinds of soils develop.

Procedure: Try to peel back the leaf litter in layers that represent a year's worth of litter. You should be able to see a noticeable difference between last year's large leaves and the somewhat decomposed leaves from the previous year. You may be able to sort out several years before you get to a level where the soil particles and leaf particles are evenly mixed. Separate the layers on pieces of paper. Write down the different characteristics of each layer, looking at color, particle size, feel of the soil, and moisture content (coolness to touch). Which layers have the most creatures and mycellium? Which has the richest smell of mold and bacteria? (The odor of newly turned soil comes mostly from the operations of a kind of branching bacteria called **actinomycetes.**) Do some digging in different parts of a woodland: slopes, in deep shade, by a brook, on the edge of a field.

Trees, like many perennial plants, are "nutrient pumps" bringing nutrients up from the deep soil, using them to make leaves, then depositing the leaves on the ground in the fall. The nutrients are released by decay and reabsorbed by the surface-feeding roots of the tree.

23 Measuring Acidity

Materials:

- Red cabbage
- Cooking pot
- Water
- Heating element (stove)
- Assorted glass containers

Background: The chemical measure of acidity in water and soils has a great effect on what can grow and live there. Changes in the degree of acidity can effectively poison some of the plants and animals whose loss will alter the entire ecosystem. Industrial pollution has increased the acidity of atmospheric particles; this acidifies not only the rain and snow but also the habitats on which the acid precipitation falls. By measuring and monitoring the degree of acidity (measured as pH) in your study area, you can gain an insight into why certain plants and animals are or are not found there.

By measuring the pH of water, you can tell the acidity of rainfall, snowfall, ponds, or streams. You can compare rain acidity that blows in from different directions, of surface waters over a year, or in changes over a number of years.

By measuring the pH of soils, you can compare acidity of different depths, areas, the changes in leaves as they break down, or the effect of rainfall on soils.

Procedure: This activity can be done indoors using a homemade solution to measure acidity of soil samples, or the solution can be taken along for on-site testing. Preparation of the indicator solution requires cooking and straining.

Preparation of the Indicator Solution: Tear or cut the leaves of a small red (i.e., purple-colored) cabbage into small pieces, put into a non-aluminum saucepan, cover with water, and heat until the cabbage leaves look pale grey and the water is strongly colored. After cooling, pour the solution into a sealable container, straining out the cabbage leaves. The cabbage pigment contains anthocyanin, which will change color when added to various materials, depending on whether they are basic (sweet or alkaline) or acid. To get an idea of how it works, pour some indicator solution into a clear glass. (A white plastic ice-cube tray with separated units also makes a good display.) Experiment with additions of small amounts of vinegar (an acid) and baking soda or ammonia (a base) to observe the reactions of the indicator.

You can make a set of colors that correspond to the standardized pH scale. Find out what colors your indicator solution makes when mixed with the substances listed below. Then, when you are testing materials from your study area, their colors

can be matched with your set of solutions with known pH to give you an approximate pH number for your sample. The indicator pigment is light sensitive and will fade in a day or so, so make a fresh batch of known solutions each time you need to measure a collection of samples.

The stronger an acid, the lower its pH. Vinegar has a pH of 2.2 (the actual pH of rainfall on mountains in North Carolina—that's acid rain!). Normal rainfall should be around a pH of 5.6; distilled water is a neutral 7.0. If soils or water are from an area where there are deposits of limestone, the reading will be more basic, around a pH of 8.0. Baking soda is 8.5, and ammonia is 13.0.

Select some of the following household chemicals to make a sample scale:

Vinegar—2.2	Distilled water—7.0
Apple juice—3.0	Baking soda—8.5
Coffee—4.2	Garden lime—12.4
Milk—6.6	Ammonia—13.0

Ecological Issues in Woodland Soil Conservation

If you have an opportunity to see the soils in tropical woodland, you might be surprised at the "clean" look of the forest floor. In a rain forest, the soil fungi operate so efficiently that fallen leaves are digested and recycled back into the trees through the mycorrhizae in a matter of days. This is one of the reasons that the practice of clear-cutting and burning in both rain forests and northern timberlands is so devastating to the forest ecosystem. Once the leaf litter and soil fungi are destroyed by the deep burning that follows a clear-cut operation, rain soon washes away the nutrient treasure, and the depleted soil cannot nourish the same kinds of trees that were cut down. Even if some trees are reseeded, the thick, fieldlike regrowth of same-species trees is a far cry from the rich diversity of plants and animals that an old-growth forest can support. (Tropical rainforests are the richest on the planet.) It may take hundreds of years of succession to recreate the many-layered mature woodland, and that can happen only if large islands of undisturbed and stable woodland are nearby to reintroduce the thousands of lost elements: the tree seeds, fungi, flowers, bees, mice, owls, worms, deer, and beetles.

Some woodland wildflowers are dependent on ants to disperse their seeds. A woolly patch makes the seed easy for ants to carry. Seeds dropped along the way may find new sites for growth.

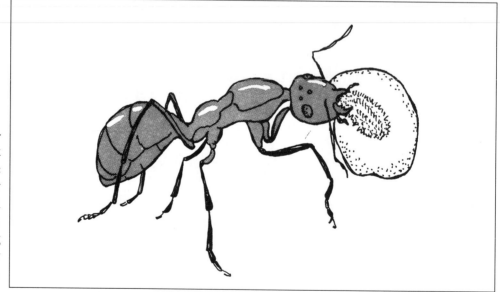

24 How You Can Affect Deforestation Practices

Background and Procedure: The issues that surround the practice of clear-cutting are complex and often decided without public knowledge. People can make a difference, however, by educating others and by changing shopping habits.

- In the United States, much of the old-growth timberland is actually owned by the public; it is in national parks and is leased to lumber companies. We even build the roads for them to go in and get the trees. Letters to senators explaining your concern for the irreplaceable ecosystem of old-growth forests will influence their decision-making process. A national environmental organization can help you with information and addresses. (See bibliography.)

- Be watchful of your use of paper and paper products. Get in the habit of using (and reusing) cloth napkins, hand towels for wipe-ups, and recycled paper products whenever possible. Find out where paper bags and newspapers can be recycled and make the effort to return them. Set up paper recycling at your school or at work.

- The cutting and burning of tropical rain forests in Central and South America is largely the result of the countries' needs to make jobs and agricultural land available to huge and impoverished populations. Local small-scale farming has always been renewable; small plots are quickly reclaimed by the surrounding forest. But large-scale cutting and burning eradicates a huge swath of forest, sending a large load of carbon dioxide into the atmosphere (contributing to the greenhouse effect)

and creating dry grassland for cattle-raising which may never be able to return to rain forest. You can involve yourself in stopping this process in several ways. Some U.S. environmental organizations are collecting funds to buy rain forest preserves. Find out if your local organizations are involved (or encourage them to be). Buy only locally produced beef (fast-food hamburgers may be from South America). Be shopper-wise on the goods you buy. Don't buy tropical woods such as teak, ebony, mahogany, or rosewood. Do choose products from environmentally sensitive companies that are trying to make markets for goods that come from rain forests. Do try to buy candies and nuts made from tropical trees, items made from natural rubber, and cosmetics made from rain forest plants. (Most rain forest plants cannot be grown as field plants but must live in intact rain forest ecosystems. Buying forest products supports people who need and will defend the forests.)

25 Identifying Environmental Stress

Background and Procedure: The effect of pollutants on the environment is often clearly seen through their impact on the health, growth, and beauty of trees. Look at trees in your area for indicators of air or water pollution. Early color changes and die-back on main branches are common in stressed trees. Limbs stressed by insect damage or fungal diseases, for instance, are likely to change color earlier than the rest of the tree. If a whole tree changes color before others nearby of the same species, a larger environmental problem may be present. Many trees along roadsides experience poisoning from salting during winter storms or exhaust poisoning from gasoline engines. The resulting stress can lead to increased insect and viral diseases (galls and deformities) and early leaf fall.

Because whole forests have sickened and begun to die over the past decades, we need to pay attention. The woodlands of mountain tops are the most vulnerable:

Trees that look permanently windblown with branches growing mostly in the direction from which the wind *doesn't* blow are actually being pruned by nature. Buds probably form on both windward and leeward sides of the tree, but strong winds dry out the buds that face the wind, and only the protected buds have a chance to grow.

They grow where they are the first to suffer the atmospheric effects of smokestack pollution, which disperses as acid smog and acid rain. These problems are complicated, but they are the results of human activities and as such can be limited so as to prevent or lessen environmental damage. Trees are not the only organisms at risk; people all over the world are being affected by the same conditions killing the trees. Localized increases in skin cancers, genetic defects, and lung diseases are signals to humans that habits must change. The following actions can help reduce environmental pollutants:

- Use cars less; use your bike and your feet more.

- Use less electricity so that less fossil fuels (gas, oil, and coal) have to be burned. That means turn out unneeded lights, use less hot water, use fewer appliances, minimize your use of air conditioners, and lower the thermostat a few degrees in winter.

- Check with your municipal road maintenance department about its use of road salt in winter. They will probably be reluctant to jeopardize public safety, but they may be willing to reduce the salt proportions in particular areas if you can point out specific damage to trees. Some towns have special stipulations for areas deemed "scenic areas," and you might be able to get an area designated for reduced winter salting.

- The increased solar radiation that has resulted in stressed mountain trees and the need for increased use of sunscreen in people is related to the use of certain industrial chemicals. These chemicals actually destroy the high atmospheric layer of ozone that protects us from harmful ultraviolet radiation. As the pollutants destroy this protective layer, we become more at risk for dangerous sunburn and skin cancers.

    The polluting gases are usually released during manufacturing processes, and they can be minimized either by recycling the materials or by simply not making them. The gases known as chlorofluorocarbons (CFCs) are particularly destructive. CFCs are used most commonly as propellants in aerosol sprays, coolants in air conditioners, and as an important ingredient in styrofoam products. Boycott or strictly limit your use of these products. Write to companies that use styrofoam pieces for packaging and tell them you won't buy from them again if they continue to use styrofoam. Don't buy clothing that has to be dry-cleaned. CFCs are released in the process of dry cleaning. (You knew already it was a toxic process just by the smell!)

26 Watch a Tree Grow

Background and Procedure: As you get to know more about the trees that live around you, choose some favorite species to plant around your home or school. If you use native species, the native creatures will get more use out of the tree, and you'll probably have fewer pests. If you can't plant a tree, choose one from your neighborhood to watch through the seasons. Let others know that you've got a special tree to watch, tell them what you have observed, and encourage them to choose their own tree to watch.

"Exploring nature with your child is largely a matter of becoming receptive to what lies all around you. It is learning again to use your eyes, ears, nostrils, and fingertips, opening the disused channels of sensory impression. For most of us, knowledge of our world comes largely through sight, yet we look about with such unseeing eyes that we are partially blind. One way to open your eyes to unnoticed beauty is to ask yourself, 'What if I had never seen this before? What if I knew I would never see it again?'"

— RACHEL CARSON, *A Sense of Wonder*

Dry Zones

DESERTS, DUNES, SANDLOTS,

AND SIDEWALKS

L ike many of our rare habitats, the dry zones have special lessons to teach us. Under dry (or xeric) conditions, each successful plant and animal must have some way to store or reduce its need for water. Dry zones are often rich in resources: plenty of sunlight, plenty of mineral nutrients, and plenty of room. The rare element is water. (And without water to carry the nutrients into an organism, nutrients are also precious.) A dry zone ecosystem is an eloquent statement on adaptations for survival where water and nutrients are limited. This chapter considers these adaptations of dry zone inhabitants and the value of preserving rare habitats.

Characteristics of the Area

Sandy soils in a dry zone feel gritty between your fingers when you pinch and rub a bit. Pieces of dead leaves and twigs rest unrotted on the surface of the land, caught in little piles under bushes or around tufts of grass. There is little leafy humus to soften the soil and no loamy smell. A handful of sandy soil crumbles easily if squeezed. Even without disturbing the soil, you can tell by the look of the plants that the soil in which they grow does not hold water very long. The plants look scrawny, with thin or tough-feeling leaves. The leaves may be densely clustered, hugging the ground, or small and sparsely placed. With few leaves covering the surface, the doings of ants and other ground animals are easy to observe.

Your study site may be a true desert, with limited rainfall and highly adapted plants such as yucca, cacti, and sagebrush. It might be the sandy dunes of the seacoast or inland lakes, where the rainfall drains too quickly through the sand to support the grasses or woodlands that flourish elsewhere in the area. An old gravel pit can be a great place to learn about dry zone ecosystems. You can also be on the

A dry zone made by human activity.

lookout for small-scale study sites; the middle of an unpaved driveway or the sandy strip between a brick wall and a sidewalk will have ants, ant lions, and plants that have many dry zone adaptations. Wintertime creates a kind of dry time in northern North America. Plants and animals that survive the season of frozen water have many of the adaptations typical in true dry zones.

Other dry zones include arctic tundra, rainshadow mountain slopes, chaparral, and acid bogs. On the arctic tundra strong winds and freezing temperatures make usable water scarce. Tops of tall mountains, especially in northern areas, also have tundralike zones that support arctic plant communities. In some mountain areas moisture-carrying clouds are cooled as they rise over the mountaintops, causing rain to fall mostly on the windward slopes. The other "rainshadow" slopes, lacking the rainfall, are likely to be dry zones protected from the rain by the height of the ridge. A chaparral is an area on the dry coastal zone of southwestern North America where limited yearly rainfall is unable to sustain forested habitat. Here the land is characterized by shrubby oaks or pines and drought-resistant herbs and grasses. In acid bogs water is plentiful but so acid that it has the effect of pulling water *out* of the roots of plants (just as a cucumber becomes limp in a solution of vinegar). Many bog plants show water-saving adaptations similar to those of desert plants.

Common Inhabitants

The following plants and animals are commonly found in most of the dry zone habitats of North America. If the area you study does not have all of these species, look for similar species and relationships that might be there.

PLANTS	ANIMALS
In Small Dry Zones	**In Small Dry Zones**
Evening primrose	Tiger beetle
Lichen	Ants
Artemesia	Ant lion larva
Mullein	Mockingbird
Lupine	Mourning dove
Sweet Fern	Spider wasp
Oak	Trapdoor spider
Pitch pine/ Pinyon pine	
	In Large Desert Ecosystems
In Large Desert Ecosystems	Gopher tortoise
Cactus	Vulture
Sagebrush	Coyote
Yucca	
Tumbleweed	
Scrub oak	
Creosote bush	

Relationships to Look for

Ant lions and ants. In the sandy areas where ants live and hunt, the ant lion lays ambush. The ant lion is a pincer-headed, soft-bodied larva that will grow up to be a long-winged flier. In its larval days it is a skillful digger of sand pits, using its long pinchers and flat head to flip sand several inches away. By tossing steadily, it creates a pit in the loose sand. Any small ant that tries to crawl across the pit is carried by the falling sand into the ant lion's jaws. Once captured, the ant lion drags its prey farther down into the sand, eats it, then returns to its position in its pit, tossing the ant husk out over the rim.

HOW TO FIND ANT LIONS

Pits can be found in fine sand under trees, on the sides of pavement, or along the edges of buildings. To see the ant lion in action, drop a small ant into one of the larger pits and look for spurts of sand as the ant lion deepens the pit, drawing its prey to the bottom. To see the larva itself, scoop up the sand that makes the pit and spread it carefully on a piece of paper. The ant lion will be still for a short time, then will try to dig away by backing. Gently blow the sand away for a good look, then return the lion to a good place for a pit. (You can put the ant lion on your hand instead of on paper; it won't hurt you, but you might be startled at the strength of the creature as it tries to burrow backwards between your fingers.)

Lupine seeds and water. For plants that live in habitats where moist growing conditions are rare or infrequent, it would be a great advantage to have some device by which the seeds would sprout only when conditions were moist enough to sustain early growth. Lupines have evolved just such a feedback system. Lupine seeds have a thick coat that seals the inner embryo and its food supply from both hungry creatures and water. Before the embryo can grow, that hard covering must be thinned. In the natural course of dry zone events, the coat might become eaten away by soil organisms that live only in moist situations or be chipped and worn by being tumbled along in a rainwater runoff. In either situation, the thinning of the coat is a signal to the embryo that conditions are good for growth. The seeds that stay encased have the ability to remain viable, ready to grow, for long periods, on the chance that conditions might change.

HOW TO FIND LUPINES

Various species of lupine grow in dry habitats from coast to coast. Each has bushy leaves in clusters of leaflets and tall stalks of flowers. Native species grow in prairies, sand dunes, deserts, and along railroad tracks. The introduced garden lupine is a long-lasting perennial that freely seeds into grassy meadows. Seeds often ripen at the base of the tall flower stalk even as the last blossoms are opening at the top. The furry, beanlike pods twist apart when the seeds are ripe, scattering the seeds away from the parent plant. Any brown seed will be ripe enough to show the attributes of the hard coat. You might want to experiment with the differences between the sprouting times of treated seeds (nick with a knife or thin by sanding) and untreated seeds.

Lichens: a relationship between fungi and algae. Every form of lichen—the ones that look like paint splotches, the ones that look like dry cereal, the tiny forests, or the brittle beards—are made up of two plants living together. Fungi threads, or **hyphae,** weave together to form a container for an inner layer of algae. Algae cells are able to photosynthesize and, in the presense of fungi, secrete extra nutrients that are consumed by the fungus host. Each lichen is made up of a specific fungi that has successfully "lichenized" a compatible algae, and experiments indicate that the eco-logical relationship we call the lichen exists only when the normally parasitic fungi is kept from consuming the algae by defensive chemicals evolved by the algal cells.

HOW TO FIND LICHENS

Lichens are found where no other plants can grow and are often indicators of this environmental condition. There are tree bark lichens, tree branch lichens, rock lichens, and bare soil lichens. A kind of yellow lichen in the Rocky Mountains can indicate a dropping-rich bird perch; a different yellow lichen on the Eastern sea coast occurs where calcium is available. An absence of lichens where lichens should be is an indicator of air pollution.

Survival in the Dry Zone

Drought, wind, and fluctuating temperatures combine in the dry zone to create a set of conditions that challenges the growth of vulnerable offspring and the maintenance of unprotected tissues. In past eons, if an environment dried gradually and the selective processes of evolution had a chance to work, some individuals were able to survive because of chance characteristics that protected them and gave them the opportunity to reproduce. Surviving offspring that inherited the beneficial characteristics of their parents or happened to be born with other adaptive attributes were able to thrive.

Evolution is an ongoing process. As long as the species exists as a healthy breeding population, each generation of varied individuals is an array of new possibilities. Under slowly changing conditions (such as continental drift, gradual warming, or a geological barrier that separates members of a population), the defining characteristics of a species, whatever characteristics help it to survive, become common in the population. Our hands and brains and the eyes with which we see the world are all the result of the same processes of selection and adaptation that have created every species of creature and plant.

As wonderful as they appear, however, no adaptation is perfect, and none can completely protect an organism or even a species from rapid changes in the current environment, especially the destructive and sometimes irreversible changes that humans are creating.

1 Why Is It Dry?

Materials:

- Paper and pen or pencil

Background: Many human practices lead to what is known as **desertification** of land that once supported complex forests (and diverse grasslands). Clearing of woody plants for fuel, lumber, charcoal-making, agriculture, or housing has resulted in the erosion of topsoil, the compaction of subsoil, and the reduced capacity of the soil to retain water. Deserts, in some form, are all around us.

Procedure: As you observe your study area, determine the reasons that might account for its dryness. Which of the following drying actions are at work? Combinations of these conditions may influence any one dry zone. Make notes on what you observe.

- Heat from sunlight evaporates available moisture.

- Rainwater runs off. Soils are shallow, underlaid with clay or bedrock, or else covered by pavement.

- An abundance of steady wind evaporates surface moisture.

- Water is abundant, but too salty, too acid, or too high in other mineral solutions to be useful to most plants.

- General weather pattern includes long periods with little or no rain.

- The soil is predominantly sandy. Without moisture-holding leaf mold, most of the water trickles down and away. This might be an overall condition (a desert) or a temporary one (loamy topsoil has been eroded, exposing the sand or clay subsoil).

- Dry atmosphere. If the moisture content of the air is low, surface moisture evaporates from the soil, plants, and animals.

You'll know which of the conditions apply to your area by using your senses and the knowledge you already have about the area. Look for exposed bedrock, compare nearby habitats, look for salty rime on stones, feel for heat or dryness on the soil surface. Look under rocks bigger than your hand for moisture or moisture-sensitive invertebrates (worms, millipedes, pill bugs, etc.). By digging into the soil, even a few inches with a stout twig or stone, you will gain some insight into the characteristics of dry zone ecosystems.

Try some of the following activities for a keener understanding of xeric (dry) conditions.

2 How Much Water Can the Soil Retain?

Materials:

- Metal can (coffee or soup) with both ends removed
- Water (about a gallon)
- Measuring cup
- Watch with a second hand

Background: Lack of moisture in the soil is the greatest limitation to plant growth. Water's role in plant growth is threefold: It transports the nutrients used to construct tissues; it is necessary for the manufacture of sugars and proteins; and it helps to maintain structure (think of a neglected houseplant or wilted cut flowers or lettuce). If the soil is mostly clay or if the area is paved, water will either run off or sit in puddles until it evaporates. In soil with a high proportion of sand and gravel, the water percolates down, out of the reach of roots, until it hits a clay or bedrock layer. In either situation, only plants with adaptations to drought can survive.

Procedure: You can test the permeability of your soil to water by doing a simple test. Push one end of the can firmly against the surface of the soil, just deeply enough so that water can flow down into the soil without escaping through the bottom rim. Pour a measured unit of water into the can and begin timing as soon as the water hits the soil. Record how long it takes for the water surface soak into the soil. You'll get a better sense of how soil texture affects water absorption if you try the test in several areas where the soils are different. Be sure to use the same procedure and the same amount of water each time. Try doing the test in exactly the same place a second time. What result do you expect? Can soil get "filled" with water? How do the results resemble natural events? What will happen to the extra water in a filled or saturated system? (Some will run off, but you will also see evidence in the reduced but continued absorption rate that the soil remains permeable.)

3 Measuring Temperature Variations

Materials:

- Household thermometer

Background: Any open land area that is exposed to the sun and sky is likely to have greater fluctuations in temperature over a twenty-four-hour period than is a habitat with dense vegetation or bodies of water. Woodlands and ponds, for instance, absorb and release heat slowly, so temperatures at ground level are less extreme. Deserts are known for hot days and chilly nights, a dangerous situation for plants and cold-blooded animals like snakes and lizards. The animals can gain control over their environment by moving to a more comfortable location, but plants have to take it as it comes and only plants with adaptations both to heat and cold can survive.

In the Sonoran Desert, a midday temperature of 100° F can drop to 20° at night; most North American plants would be killed by such a change. Though many species of plants can survive extremes in temperature, the change must be gradual. For example, many evergreens, such as rhododendrons or pines, can survive temperatures below zero during a cold winter. Their greatest stress occurs on a warm, sunny day in early spring when a sudden cold wind quickly drops the temperature of a sun-warmed leaf.

Procedure: You can find out more about the ranges of temperature in the soil of your study area if you test the soil at various times of the day or year.

Experiment with your thermometer before you do your explorations. See how long it takes for the column of mercury to level off to its final reading. Find out the difference in temperature when you place the thermometer on the ground facing the sun (the air temperature at ground level) and when you place the thermometer's bulb against the soil and cover it with a layer of insulation (a sock or piece of foam) so that the temperature of the soil, not the air, is being measured. Is there a further difference if you bury the bulb of the thermometer in the ground? (*Never* push the thermometer itself into the soil; dig a hole with a tool or stick or use a natural hole. The glass tube is easily broken, and the mercury inside is poisonous.)

If you are working with others, make sure your thermometers give the same reading for the same place. Sometimes the glass tube can be *carefully* slid up or down on the backing to standardize the instruments. Talk about what general question you want to answer about temperature variations in your area. (For instance, do you want to find out about the relationship of air to soil temperatures, the range of air temperatures, or the effect of direct sunlight on surface temperatures?) Decide on the procedures that will best answer your question.

You will also need to decide whether you will use the centigrade (C) or Fahrenheit (F) scale for your records. The centigrade scale is better for understanding how near freezing (0° C) the temperature is, but the Fahrenheit scale is more commonly used in the United States, and most Americans are likely to know how 60° F feels. Decide which is more helpful to you, and use only that scale. Use the following worksheet to record your observations.

Location:_____ Date:_____ Weather Conditions:_____

General description of the habitat: _____

_____

_____

Question you want to answer:_____

_____

_____

LOCATION	PROCEDURE	RESULTS

Site 1:_____

_____

_____

Site 2:_____

_____

_____

Site 3:_____

_____

_____

Site 4:_____

_____

_____

Make the following comparisons as you investigate the temperature variables in your study area.

- Find the warmest and coolest spots in your study area. Once you have pinpointed them, predict where other warm and cool spots will occur by comparing plant species or soils with the areas you have tested.

- In what area do you think the temperatures will change the most between daytime and nighttime? Check it out.

4 The Effects of Wind

Materials:

- 3- or 4-foot stick (yardstick)
- Yarn or kite string (at least a yard)
- Protractor or card with lines indicating 30°, 45°, 60°, and 90° angles.

Background: A dry zone habitat is often a place of moving air. If the soil is fully exposed to direct sun, then the heated, rising air creates currents that work to evaporate moisture. In mountainous and coastal areas vegetation grows close to the surface or in protected situations away from the drying effect of strong wind. Upward-seeking, exposed stems become dessicated and cells die, especially on the sides that face the wind. But even in the windiest areas, air flow just above the soil is reduced by physical irregularities and by the wind's rebounding from the ground against its own force. Coupled with the modifying effect of heat-retentive rocks and soil, the atmosphere of the first several inches above the ground is much more hospitable to living organisms. Nonetheless, blowing sand or snow may scour away plants in a dry zone. If you are studying such a dry zone, you can probably see that the plants that survive there have most of their leaves growing in protected places—close to the earth and perhaps in arrangements like tufts, sprawling mats, or rounded rosettes that help cut down on water loss due to wind.

A plant that grows in the shape of a round cushion has a better chance of surviving the stressful conditions of life in a dry zone. Its survival makes it possible for other animals to exist—notice the tracks.

Procedure: You can test the power of wind at various heights from the ground. (Choose a windy day to do your experiment.) Tie lengths of yarn or string to a stick or yardstick at 6-inch intervals. At least 5 inches of yarn should dangle freely from each indicator. As the wind blows, compare the wind's ability to lift the indicators away from their resting position. A card marked with angles might help you record your observations. For instance, a 90° movement would indicate a strong wind. Try the experiment several times and during different weather conditions. Do you see any correlations between the strength of the wind in your area and the growth habits of the plants?

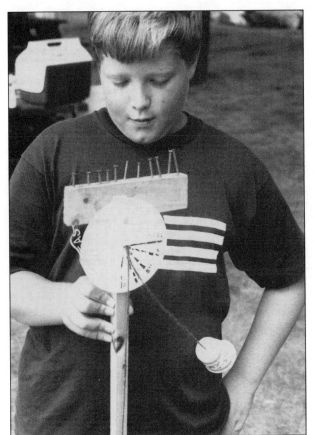

A wind-speed indicator can be made from commonly found materials.

5 How Dry Zone Leaves Conserve Moisture

Materials:

- Paper towel (or coffee filter paper)
- Scissors
- Two or more same-sized glasses or small jars
- Water

Background: The principal function of a plant's leaves is to catch light for the production of sugars and proteins. As solar energy is captured by the green chloroplasts within plant tissues, water is utilized and released, which pulls additional water from roots or storage cells. Water moves out of the plant through pores in the underside of the leaves. Sunlight triggers the pores to open and water flows out as vapor. Too much heat and too much light speeds up the process to the point of jeopardizing the life of the plant, creating a water deficit in the stems and roots.

The plants that are adapted to survive the combination of direct sunlight and limited fresh water have one or more of the following characteristics:

- Leaf shape is thin (grasslike) or with narrow margins along branching veins. In strong sunlight, enough sugar can be manufactured by the small amount of green tissue. A small surface area reduces the chance of overheating, and few pores limits water loss.

- Leaves are nonexistent or else ephemeral, sprouting only when water is available in the soil. This adaptation is used primarily by woody plants and helps them survive extended dry periods.

- Leaves tilt sideways or curl at the edges. Heat damage is reduced by angling away from the midday sunlight. Curling or folding shades the pores from sunlight and protects them from the wind.

- Undersides or pore-bearing surfaces are furry, light-colored, or deeply recessed, reducing water loss because of limited exposure to sun or wind movement.

- Leaf covering restricts amount of sunlight. Shiny or whitish surfaces reflect light. Waxy coating seals in moisture. Hairiness provides shading for inner tissues. Red pigments, especially in cool, high altitude habitats, are produced in response to stress, reducing cell damage from intense radiation.

- Leaf tissue has water storage cells, giving leaves a thick appearance.

- Oils inside the leaf reduce evaporation. (Think of all the dry zone, or xerophylic, cooking herbs, known for their strong-smelling oils: thyme, lavender, rosemary, and sage).

- Leaves are arranged in compact spirals called rosettes. The rosette's round shape and slightly overlapping leaves protect the leaves from drying conditions while allowing every leaf to absorb sunlight.

Leaves that show dry zone adaptations

Procedure: How do these adaptations help a plant conserve water? Try experimenting with how the shape of a leaf affects the evaporation of water from its surface. Cut your "leaf" out of paper towel or filter paper. Your model must have a "stem" of paper long enough to reach into the water in your container. As water evaporates from the paper model, more water will be drawn up from the supply in the container. By comparing the amounts of water remaining in the jars, you can get an idea of which leaf shapes best conserve water.

For your first experiment, make two leaves of equal length, but make one thinner than the other. Place the stems of the models in equal amounts of water and in the same sunny (or windy) location. After an hour or so (depending on the weather), compare the water levels. Try to come up with other materials or techniques for making models that would help you test other dry zone adaptations.

6 Defense Tactics

Materials:

- Pencils, crayons, or markers
- Paper

Background: All of the adaptations to drought protection listed in the previous activity also protect the plants from consumption by animals. But leaves are at a premium in the sparse vegetation of the dry zones, and many creatures have special adaptations for overcoming the tough or furry armor of these plants. Over the course of evolutionary time, the fight for survival escalates: The animals that survive are better at attacking and the plants that survive are better at defending. As a result, the defenses of desert plants are impressive. Here are some of their special defense adaptations:

- Sticky saps and resins that ooze out of a bite wound, both sealing the gash and gumming up the mouth-parts of the aggressor.

- Alkaloid chemicals in the sap that slow down the animal's digestive processes, perhaps even slowing down growth to the extent that an insect would be unable to complete its life cycle before cold weather.

- Pungent oils that taste or smell bad to casual grazers.

- Spikes, thorns, prickles, bristles, and dense hairs that deter any tender-mouthed consumers.

Procedure: Make a list of the ways various animals protect themselves from predators (consider skunks, cats, woolly caterpillars, toads, or tortoises). Use your observations to create adaptations for an imaginary plant that protects itself. Draw your plant and its predator.

7 How Plants Affect the Dry Zone

Materials:

- Notebook
- Pen or pencil

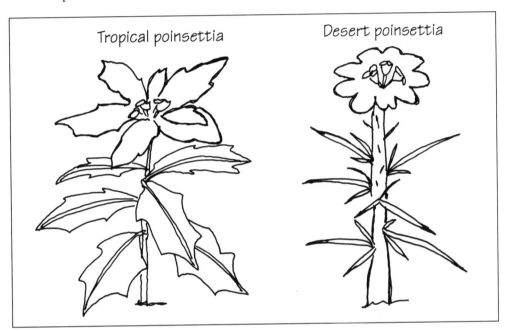

Background: Every plant affects its environment. While it is coping with wind, it is slowing the wind down. While it is dealing with sun, it is creating some shade. By flowering, it feeds insects. By making seeds, it is producing offspring. By dying, it is making room for other plants and adding nutrients to the soil.

Procedure: Look around and see if you can find ways that growing plants are making habitats for other plants and animals. Choose two plants to observe. Describe each plant (name if possible) and record the answers to the following questions:

1. Does the growth habit of the plant let it catch and hold dead leaves around its base?

_____

_____

(The leaves act as a mulch, keeping the soil moist and enhancing decay and release of mineral nutrients.)

2. Are young plants growing under the protection of the branches of your plant?

_____

_____

Do you think the new plants will eventually change the growing conditions of the "nurse" plant?

_____

_____

3. Does the plant have a special adaptation for dealing with limited water supplies?

_____

_____

(Some plants have a long, central root called a taproot, which penetrates down to deep water and may have water storage tissues. Biennials such as evening primrose and perennials such as cacti have taproots. Other plants may have a wide-ranging network of fine rootlets.)

4. Is the soil bare around your plant?

_____

_____

(Some plants secrete toxins that poison the seedlings of would-be competitors for precious soil moisture. Evertgreen plants may shade out most seedling competitors.)

8 Look at a Cactus—But Not Too Closely!

Materials:

- Actual cactus plants or photos of cacti

Background: Cacti seem to be the epitome of the dry zone survivor. Tender leaves have turned into protective spikes; thick stems have taken over photosynthesis and act as water storage areas at the same time. Many cacti have root systems that combine deep taproots for the mining and storing of water with a wide-flung fibrous network of roots that collect rainfall just below the soil surface. A naturally occurring dry zone would not be complete without some species of cactus; in fact, every state has records of native cacti. They grow in sand dunes, dry grasslands, coastal piney woods, seashores, dry mountain slopes, and, of course, deserts.

Cactus plants also provide shelter and food for a wide variety of animals. Hawks nest on their tops, woodpeckers and owls nest inside them, and songbirds and rodents find safety in their thorny arms. Somehow, tortoises eat their stems, while other species feast first upon in the nectar from their flowers and then upon their fruits and seeds. The cactus is a central unit in the flow of desert life.

The cactus wren of the Southwest uses the formidable defense tactics of the cholla cactus to protect its own offspring.

Where did cacti come from? Geological records say that deserts were once forests and grasslands. What did a cactus plant look like then, before it became a cactus, before the increasingly drying climate eliminated all offspring that couldn't cope? Some botanists say a cactus evolved from a family of plants that is now found only in tropical rain forests. The leaves may be very different among plants of the same family; it is in the similarities among flowers that the ancestry of a plant is traced. A plant's flowers change the least over time, while the body of the plant—the shapes of its leaves, stems, and roots—is altered by the stepping-stone process of chance mutations and selection of beneficial characteristics.

Procedure: Select an example of a cactus, either an actual plant or a good photograph of one, and observe all its dry zone adaptations. Compare types of cacti for shared or different characteristics. Can you match its flowers with examples of rainforest flowers?

9 Animals That Live in the Dry Zone

Materials:

- Pencils, crayons, or markers
- Drawing paper
- Pictures of familiar, nondesert animals (insects, birds, amphibians, etc.)

Background and Procedure: How do you think an animal would look and act that could live in a place with temperature extremes, sparse, tough vegetation, not much water, and few places to hide? Consider each of the following attributes of dry zone animals. Then choose an animal that does not live in a dry zone and draw a picture showing the modifications it would need to survive in a desert area. Give your new animal a name.

- **Color.** Many desert-living creatures are camouflaged to match the light-hued, sandy background, but some are an unlikely solid black, the color most able to make its wearer hot. Cold overnight temperatures cause problems for dry zone animals, especially for those with small bodies or no way to heat themselves internally (insects, reptiles, spiders). In the morning, when the chill of the night is still making movement difficult for such creatures, a black body absorbs warmth quickly from the sunlight. During maximum heat times, the black coloring is dangerous, and shade or a deep hole must be sought.

- **Shape.** In a hot, dry climate small size, long, thin limbs, and large ears with many blood vessels to bring body heat to the surface help release extra body heat. A big, chunky body with small ears conserves body heat and describes the shape most commonly found in arctic mammals.

- **Behavior.** If the dry conditions result from high temperatures, the ability to create or find cooler quarters during the hottest hours is crucial, especially for **ectotherms,** the lizards, snakes, toads, and arthropods who cannot cool or heat their bodies through metabolic processes. Taking cover under rocks or in some shade is an essential behavior for these animals and an energy-saving behavior of mammals and birds. The behavior of one species may also affect the survival of another. Desert tortoises play an important role in the lives of many other species by providing deep tunnels into the cooler, moister layers of sand. Areas where the tortoise population has been reduced by human practices of habitat destruction and snake hunts (killing rattlesnakes by gassing tortoise tunnels) has also reduced the populations of a variety of other species that could otherwise survive in the many protective tunnels made by the tortoises.

- **Protective adaptations.** Prey animals are especially vulnerable in open dry zone areas. Speed is a handy adaptation for them. Consider the quickness of most

Jackrabbit

Eastern cottontail

The lanky limbs and long ears of the jackrabbit of desert habitats help the animal cool off its blood before it returns to the body. The stubbier legs and ears of the cottontail rabbit function to help retain heat, an important way to save energy during cold weather.

lizards, jackrabbits, kangaroo rats. The slower prey animals have other techniques, including noxious sprays (skunks, bombardier beetles), camouflage to resemble their background or actual objects such as sticks, leaves, or bird droppings (moths, caterpillars, toads, lizards), armor (tortoises), a noxious taste (fireflies, monarch butterflies), stings (scorpions and ants).

- **Predator behaviors.** A predator must have its own adaptations to overcome the defense tactics of the prey. They must move even faster than the fast-running prey.

Ecologists have observed coyotes and badgers traveling together while hunting. The coyote benefits by grabbing animals flushed by the digging badger; the badger may benefit by getting prey that have been frightened into staying underground by the presence of the coyote.

Think of roadrunners, coyotes, tiger beetles, and the quick-eyed spider wasps. Those that don't rely on speed have other tactics. Ant lion larvae dig sand pits as traps. Rattlesnakes can kill by delivering a single, poisonous bite from ambush. Trapdoor spiders hide inside a silk-lined hole under a disk of soil that serves as a trapdoor for unsuspecting prey. Ants, Harris hawks, crows, and coyotes work cooperatively in extended family groups. The amount of actual "communicating" varies with the species, but working together instead of competing individually benefits more offspring, especially in a dry zone ecosystem.

Endangered Desert Ecosystems

Creatures become rare when their habitat becomes rare, threatened when their support system is threatened. Despite a beautifully interlocking ecosystem of wonderfully adapted plants and animals, a desert is a fragile place. Physical damage to the topsoil is not readily healed by rapidly growing or weedy plant species. Though desert species are well-adapted to their difficult environment, they do have limits in their tolerence of dessication and high temperature. Any radical change can cause a collapse of the ecosystem. Even when the habitat is protected and stabilized, if the area is isolated and too small to support a large breeding population of varying individuals, inbreeding may undermine the health of the species. Evolution, which is the means by which a species continues into the future, operates through variations in the species. Inbreeding limits the possibilities.

Homeless Hummers

Hummingbirds, common residents of our southwestern desert areas, are good examples of creatures that become rare when ecosystems are endangered. They are important pollinators of many dry zone flowering plants, although their diet also includes insects. During the winter months, most hummers move south to tropical woodlands where nectar and insects are abundant. Although some hummingbirds can migrate long distances without stopping (ruby-throated hummingbirds make a 500-mile nonstop flight over water), most need frequent refills of sugar and protein (insects) to fuel their long journey. When tropical and desert habitats are destroyed, hummers lose both refueling stations and the sustaining habitats at both ends of their journey.

10 How Can We Help Save Threatened Habitats?

Background and Procedure: Few organisms can adapt fast enough to survive the rapid pace of human changes, and we are now wiping out rare habitats and rare species at a reckless rate. We do not know in what ways our environment will change, nor can we predict how plants and animals will evolve to create the ecosystems of the future. Scientists are now beginning a systematic study of which species can fulfill which of our needs; humans are finally recognizing that it is foolhardy and short-sighted to allow habitats to be destroyed just because we can't at this moment state their importance to us.

Our understanding of the value and complexity of ecosystems is still a fledgling science. Even more undeveloped is a worldwide public appreciation of how future human welfare depends on a diverse and stable global ecosystem. Here are some of the things you can do to help:

- *Support local and international efforts to save land from development.* The protection of any rare species is totally dependent on the preservation of its rare habitat. Raising young in captivity or storing seeds in seedbanks (cool, dry, artificial conditions) is a last-ditch or backup situation. The land and any of the ecosystems that relate to it must be protected if an endangered species of plant or animal is to survive. You can help by joining organizations, by raising money to help them further, and by speaking out and writing letters to express your support.

- *Don't buy products made from endangered species or taken from threatened ecosystems.* If no one buys the ivory from elephants or whales, their illegal slaughter will stop. If no one buys salad bowls of teak, mahogany, or rosewood, these slow-growing tropical hardwoods won't be cut down. Do buy products that support good stewardship practices. Many renewable resources can be harvested from the rain forests without destroying the ecosystem. The sale of natural rubber products and tropical nuts such as cashews and Brazil nuts encourages the care and preservation of the world's precious rain forests. Money is a powerful motivator; spend yours wisely.

- *Try to educate others.* There is a common rumor that support of environmental policies may cost some people their jobs. Few people are willing to lose their livelihoods, even if their job is part of a destructive process. If you are beginning to think about a career, set your sights on work that doesn't hurt the earth. If you have a job in an industry that might be hurting the environment, use your political power and your knowledge of the processes to help heal the problems created by short-sighted operations.

What Can Be Learned from Local Dry Zone Ecology?

If you have been studying an area that has become dry recently due to lumbering activities, fire, surface mining, or agriculture, you probably noticed that the plants and animals of your area can also be found in other habitats. The species in your study area were able to survive in the dry zone when more vulnerable species died or moved as the area became drier. You will probably find that the characteristics of the survivors match those of the desert dwellers discussed in previous activities.

11 Our Dependence on Soil and Water

Materials:

- Writing materials
- A reference encyclopedia

Background: Imagine that a large farm region has become too dry to support crops. Old varieties of plants would no longer sustain humans and their livestock. Corn, wheat, soy, rice, and beans, for instance, require lots of nutrients and lots of water. How could people survive? What actions could they take?

   In many areas this scenario is not an imaginary threat. We flirt with drought situations whenever we contaminate our wells and rivers with road salts, excess lawn and farm fertilizers and pesticides, seepage from industrial wastes, and acid rain. Our air pollution is changing conditions in the upper atmosphere to such an extent that it is predicted that warming climates could reduce the rainfall over extensive areas, many of which now sustain us with grains.

Procedure: Make a list of the foods that are staple needs in your family and community. Where do the plants and animals grow that make up these foods? Are they areas where rainfall sustains the crops or is the water piped in from distant rivers or deep wells? (Check your local library for resources. You may need to inquire into the state agricultural agencies for more detailed information.) As you learn and think about our daily needs and uses of water, pay attention to which uses fit into normal water cycles and which are dependent on artificial systems.

Find out where the drinking water in your home comes from by contacting the local water company. Most of the people living in North America have water in abundance, even people in dry zones. With water so handy we forget to be careful, and much of our fresh water is wasted and contaminated needlessly. Once water is chemically contaminated, it can be reused only after it has been cleaned at great expense. If you live where water flows over the surface in the form of lakes and reservoirs, your fresh water fell as rain or snow fairly recently. Rainwater has been naturally cleaned by evaporating and then condensing into clouds. Water that comes from wells sunk deep in the ground is "old" rainwater that has slowly filtered down through permeable soil (also a cleansing process) or trickled down through cracks in the bedrock. Water moves downward until it is stopped by a layer of rock or clay. There it builds up as an area of water-soaked soil known as an **aquifer**. Deep wells that tap into aquifers are the commonest sources of water in North America's dry zones.

12　How Can Soil Hold on to Water?

Materials:

- Two drinking glasses (or similar small containers)
- Sandy soil to half-fill one container
- Loamy soil (dirt) to half-fill the other container
- A measuring cup
- Water (about a cup)

Background: Aquifer can extend over a great distance with the water entering at one site and then being transported by the spongelike permeable soil. An aquifer of water-soaked soil may extend under mountains and over a mounded layer of bedrock and can emerge as a water source at a valley hundreds of miles away.

Procedure: To see how well sandy soil holds on to water, try an experiment using two types of soil—sandy soil and loamy topsoil. Put half a cup of sandy soil in one container and half a cup of loamy soil in another container. Pour equal amounts of water (half a cup) in each soil sample, let the samples sit for about a minute, and then carefully pour the water out of each sample, measuring the amounts of unabsorbed water from each sample for comparison. Which soil holds water better? Do you have any ideas about where the sandy soil puts the water? (The water clings to each sand particle and also fills the spaces between particles.) What do you think would happen if you tried the experiment a second time with the same water-soaked materials?

13 Endangered Water Supplies

Materials:

- A clear plastic soda or shampoo bottle with its bottom removed
- A piece of screen or nylon stocking
- Sand to fill the bottle
- Water
- A clean container for catching the waste
- A selection of pollutants, including cooking oil, liquid soap, food coloring, nail polish remover

Background: Aquifers are essential water supplies for the agricultural and daily needs for many people in North America. For the people of the plains, desert zones, and many coastal islands, aquifer water is their only consistent water supply. Some aquifers that presently supply large cities and their dependent agriculture are reservoirs of water that have been accumulating for thousands of years. Because of the wide extent of an aquifer, heavy agricultural use in one part of a state may lower the level, or the **water table**, of a well somewhere else in that state, or even in the next state. In addition, underground water sources are not safely tucked away from surface pollution. Leakage from stored or dumped toxic material will eventually find its way through the layers of sand or limestone into the aquifer. It is of paramount importance, therefore, to limit the production of nuclear and other toxic wastes and to stop or tightly control and monitor the practice of dumping or storing such waste.

Our habits have created these predicaments; new habits can heal the environment.

Procedure: First make a sand filter system by covering the small end of the bottomless bottle with a piece of screening or panty hose, held in place by a rubber band or tape. Set your sand filter on some firm support and fill it with sand. You will be experimenting to find out what kinds of contaminants are filtered by the sand as the water moves down and into the catch cup.

Household contaminants find their way into underground water supplies, either by being dumped or by seeping from a septic system or a landfill. Make your own version of polluted water by adding distinctive liquids or materials that you can identify (not by tasting) if they come through the sand filter. Try mixing in some fine soil, food coloring, liquid soap (your water will foam when shaken if it contains soap), salad or cooking oil, and some cleaning fluid or nail polish remover that can be identified by smell. Be careful with your chemistry. CAUTION: DO NOT MIX CHLORINE BLEACH WITH OTHER CLEANING COMPOUNDS THAT MIGHT CONTAIN AMMONIA.

Slowly pour your polluted solution into the sand filter (save a small amount for later comparison) and observe the progression of water through the sand. Compare the filtered water in the catch cup with that of your original solution. What materials are still present? Note: In a natural soil filtering system, bacteria living in the soil would break down some of the organic materials such as sewage wastes and oils.

14 What Can Be Done to Save Water Supplies?

Materials:

- Gallon container (perhaps an open-topped milk container)
- Bathroom shower
- Paper and pencil

Background and Procedure: Taking long showers is one of the major ways we waste water in the home. You can see how much water is wasted by doing the following activity. Hold your open-topped gallon milk container under the showerhead and time how quickly it fills. Then time the showers each family member takes in one day. Calculate the amount of shower water your family uses per month:

Number of seconds to fill container: _____

Divide by 60 seconds:

(A)_____ This is the number of minutes it takes to use one gallon of water.

Number of minutes shower is used each day (combined usage by all family members):

(B)_____

Divide (B) by (A) to get the number of gallons used per day: _____

Multiply by 30 to get number of gallons used each month: _____

Get a commitment from each family member to reduce his or her shower time (suggest a 5-minute maximum). Then time them again and figure out the new monthly water-usage amount. The difference is the amount of water your family will save each month.

Here are some other ways you can conserve water in your home:

- *Pay attention to how you use water.* Run water only when you are using it. Turn it off while you brush your teeth. Don't run the kitchen faucet to get a glass of cold water; keep a water bottle in the refrigerator.

- *Water your garden by hand or use drip irrigation* (slow seeping of water through a special woven hose). Try to use plants that are native to your area for your flowers and shrubs. Reconsider the consequences of a water- and chemical-addicted perfect green lawn. Could some part of that lawn become a natural meadow for wildlife? We waste thousands of gallons of fresh water yearly in each of our attempts to maintain artificial ecosystems around our homes.

- *Study your daily water disposal habits and search for ways to reuse water.* Try to become an ecosystem. Can you capture rainwater to water your lawns or gardens? Can the water used to cook vegetables or the juice in canned vegetables be made into soup? Can you catch and store the waste water from your baths and sink to water plants or wash the car?

- *Check out your hardware store for gadgets that will help you save water.* Devices can be added to your faucets and showerheads to reduce water consumption while still providing good water pressure. Toilet tank dams can reduce the amount of water necessary for flushing. You can make your own dam by filling a plastic container with sand, sealing it carefully, and placing it in the tank so that it doesn't interfere with the working parts. Don't use bricks or other items that might put loose particles in the tank.

- *Fix all leaky faucets and toilets.* Turn off the water at the main shutoff valve, unscrew the faucet or the attachment at its end with a wrench or spanner, take out the old rubber washer, replace it with a new one of the same size from the hardware store, and you're ready to reassemble and turn the water back on. One leaky faucet can waste several thousand gallons of water over a year!

15   Keeping Our Water Pure

Background and Procedure: The last activity gave suggestions for conserving our water supply. Here are some ways we can help keep our water clean:

- *Pay attention to what you throw away.* Make sure that household cleaning products or painting materials with warnings on the labels are never thrown in the regular trash. The materials and their containers should go to a special toxic materials collection site. Better yet, don't buy them in the first place. They may work well to clean, but the cleaning power of soap, vinegar, baking soda, or ammonia may be all you need. (Check libraries for recipes for alternative cleaning solutions.) Our water supplies are at stake.

- *Be curious; be suspicious.* Illegally dumped wastes, leaking barrels of unknown fluids, or abandoned industrial sites where fuels or chemical wastes could be buried are all potential dangers to your community. If you are concerned about signs of pollution at places where plants don't grow or animals are dying, take your concerns to local EPA officials, your conservation commission, or a nearby environmental organization. (*Note:* Some "pollution" is natural. In pools or backwaters, you may see natural oil slicks from decaying vegetation, and after a vigorous rain and runoff, mountain streams can foam because of natural softening agents in soils and tree bark.)

- *Find out where your water comes from originally.* On what land does your water first fall as rain? By looking at a map or by visiting your water company you can find out what that land (your watershed) is like. Is there any development or dumping that might add some unwanted "extras" to your water? Is the land protected from development? Find out what state laws are protecting your water supply.

Bibliography

It is impossible to list all the good books on ecology; there are far too many and with the renewed interest in the topic, new books are constantly appearing. The following list includes those books that I'm confident will teach you about ecology and inspire you to learn more.

General Information and Inspiration

Bates, Marston. *The Forest and the Sea: A Look at the Economy of Nature and the Ecology of Man.* New York: Random House, 1960.

Caldicott, Helen. *If You Love This Planet: A Plan to Heal the Earth.* New York: W.W. Norton and Company, 1992.

Dillard, Annie. *Pilgrim at Tinker Creek.* New York: Bantam Books, 1978.

Ehrlich, Paul, R. *The Machinery of Nature: The Living World Around Us—And How It Works.* New York: Simon and Schuster, 1986.

Lappe, Francis Moore. *Diet for a Small Planet.* New York: Ballantine Books, 1982.

Leopold, Aldo. *A Sand County Almanac with Essays on Conservation from Round River.* New York: Ballantine Books, 1966.

Mabey, Richard. *Oak and Company.* New York: Greenwillow Books, 1983.

Odum, Eugene P. *Ecology and Our Endangered Life-Support Systems.* Sunderland, Mass.: Sinauer Associates, 1989.

Pedersen, Anne. *The Kids' Environment Book: What's Awry and Why.* Santa Fe, N.M.: John Muir Publications, 1991.

Stein, Sara. *Noah's Garden: Restoring the Ecology of Our Own Back Yards.* Boston: Houghton Mifflin, 1993.

Storer, John H. *The Web of Life: A First Book of Ecology.* New York: Mentor Books, 1953.

Watts, May Theilgaard. *Reading the Landscape of America.* New York: Collier Books, 1975.

Guides to Identification and Behavior

Audubon Society Field Guide series. New York: Chanticleer Press.

Benyus, Janine. *The Field Guide to Wildlife of the Eastern United States* and *The Field Guide to Wildlife of the Western United States.* New York: Simon and Schuster, 1989.

Covell, Charles V. *A Field Guide to the Moths of Eastern North America.* Boston: Houghton Mifflin, 1984.

Forey, Pamela and Cecilia Fitzsimons. *An Instant Guide to Butterflies.* New York: Bonanza Books, 1987.

Kress, Stephen W. *The Audubon Society Handbook for Birders: A Guide To Locating, Observing, Identifying, Recording, Photographing, and Studying Birds.* New York: Charles Scribner's Sons, 1981.

Leslie, Clare Walker. *Nature All Year Long.* Fairfield, N.J.: Greenwillow Books, 1991.

Morgan, Ann Haven. *Field Book of Ponds and Streams.* New York: Putnam's Sons, 1930.

Newcomb, Lawrence. *Newcomb's Wildflower Guide.* Boston: Little, Brown and Company, 1977.

Pasquier, Roger F. *Watching Birds: An Introduction to Ornithology.* Boston: Houghton Mifflin Company, 1977.

Peterson, Roger Tory, ed. The Peterson Field Guide Series. Boston: Houghton Mifflin Company.

Rezendes, Paul. *Tracking and the Art of Seeing: How to Read Animal Tracks and Signs.* Charlotte, Vt.: Camden House Publishing, l992.

Stokes, Donald and Lillian. Stokes Nature Guides. Boston: Little, Brown and Company.

Symond, George W. D. *The Tree Identification Book.* New York: Quill, 1958.

Tyning, Thomas F. *A Guide to Amphibians and Reptiles.* Boston: Little, Brown and Company, 1990.

Activity Books that Teach Science, Biology, Art, and Ecology

Daduto, Michael J. and Joseph Bruchac. *Keepers of the Animals: Native American Stories and Wildlife Activities for Children.* Golden, Colo.: Fulcrum Publishing, 1991.

Christensen, Karen. *Home Ecology: Simple and Practical Ways to Green Your Home.* Golden, Colo.: Fulcrum Publishing, 1990.

Cornell, Joseph. *Sharing the Joy of Nature: Nature Activities For All Ages.* Nevada City, Calif.: Dawn Publications, 1989.

Dekkers, Midas. *The Nature Book.* New York: Macmillan Publishing, 1988.

Duensing, Ed. *Talking to Fireflies, Shrinking the Moon: A Parent's Guide to Nature Activities.* New York: New American Library, 1990.

Elkington, John, Julia Hailes, Douglas Hill, and Joel Makower. *Going Green: A Handbook for Saving the Planet.* New York: Viking Press, 1990.

Earth Works Group. *50 Simple Things You Can Do to Save the Earth.* Berkeley, Calif.: Earthworks Press, 1989.

Herman, Marina L., Joseph F. Passiniau, Ann L. Schimpf, and Paul Treuer. *Teaching Kids to Love the Earth.* Duluth, Minn.: Pfeifer-Hamilton, 1991.

Hunken, Jorie. *Botany For All Ages.* Old Saybrook, Conn.: Globe Pequot, 1989.

Hunken, Jorie. *Birdwatching For All Ages.* Old Saybrook, Conn.: Globe Pequot, 1991.

Kenda, Margaret and Phyllis S. Williams. *Science Wizardry For Kids.* Hauppage, N.Y.: Barron's Educational Series, l992

Leslie, Claire Walker. *The Art of Field Sketching.* Layton, Utah: Gibbs, Smith Publishing, reprint 1993.

Lewis, Barbara A. *The Kid's Guide to Social Action: How to Solve the Social Problems You Choose—and Turn Creative Thinking into Positive Action.* Minneapolis, Minn.: Free Spirit Publishing, 1991.

Levenson, Elaine, *Teaching Children About Science.* Englewood Cliffs, N.J.: Prentice-Hall, 1985

Metzger, Mary and Cinthya P. Whittaker. *This Planet is Mine: Teaching Environmental Awareness and Appreciation to Children.* New York: Simon and Schuster, 1991.

Milord, Susan. *The Kids Nature Book: 365 Indoor/Outdoor Activities.* Charlotte, Vt: Williamson Publishing, 1989.

Nature Scope guides. National Wildlife Federation, 1400 16th St. NW, Washington, DC 20036-2266.

Nicklesberg, Janet. *Nature Activities for Early Childhood.* Reading, Mass.: Addison Wesley, 1976.

Project Learning Tree, The American Forest Council, 1250 Connecticut Ave. NW, Washington, D.C.: 1979.

Project Wild, Salina Star Route, Boulder, Colo. 80302.

Rockwell, Robert E. *Hug a Tree: And Other Things to Do Outdoors with Young Children.* Mt. Rainier, Md.: Gryphon House, 1985.

Roth, Charles E., Cleti Cervoni, Thomas Wellnitz, and Elizabeth Arms. *Beyond the Classroom: Exploration of Schoolground and Backyard.* Lincoln, Mass.: Massachusetts Audubon Society, 1991.

Russell, Helen Ross. *Ten-Minute Field Trips: Using the School Grounds for Environmental Studies.* Chicago: Ferguson, 1973.

Russo, Monica. *The Insect Almanac: A Year-Round Activity Guide.* New York: Sterling Publishing, 1992.

Schneck, Marcus. *Your Backyard Wildlife Garden: How to Attract and Identify Wildlife in Your Yard.* Emmaus, PA: Rodale Press, 1992.

Sisson, Edith A. *Nature with Children of All Ages: Activities and Adventures for Exploring, Learning, and Enjoying the World Around Us.* Englewood Cliffs, N.J.: Prentice-Hall, 1982.

Swanson, Diane. *A Toothy Tongue and One Long Foot: Nature Activities for Children.* North Vancouver, British Columbia: Whitecap Books, Ltd., 1990.

Magazines and Periodicals

Audubon Activist, National Audubon Society, 950 Third Ave., New York, NY 10022.

Buzzworm, Buzzworm, Inc., 1818 16th St., Boulder, Colo. 80302.

E Magazine, 28 Knight St., Norwalk, Conn. 06851.

Garbage: The Practical Journal for the Environment, Old House Journal Corp., 435 Ninth St., Brooklyn, NY 11215.

Natural History Magazine, The American Museum of Natural History, Central Park West at 79th St., New York, NY 10024.

Nature Study Magazine: A Journal of Environmental Education and Interpretation, The American Nature Study Society, 5881 Cold Brook Rd., Homer, NY 13077.

Organic Gardening Magazine, Rodale Press, Inc., 33 E. Minor St., Emmaus, PA 18098.

P3: The Earth-based Magazine for Kids, P3 Foundation, P.O. Box 52, Montgomery, VT 05470.

Ranger Rick, National Wildlife Federation, 1400 16th St. N.W., Washington, D.C. 20077-9955.

Index

Acid precipitation, 76, 155, 180
Ailanthus, 2, 25
   seed, 95
Algae, 49, 162
Alliances, 102
Aluminum cans, 32
Ambush bug, 81–82
Ant lion, 159, 160
Ant, 2, 14 , 20–21, 81, 101, 102, 152, 159, 160
   carpenter, 119, 144
Aphid, 14, 101–102
Aquifer, 181, 182
Artemesia, 159
Ash tree, 25
   seed, 95
Aspen miner, 138
Aster, 81

Backswimmer, 60, 62
Badger, 178
Bagworm, 2–4
Baiting, at the water's edge, 66
Bark beetle, 119, 121–22
Bee fly, 81
Beech, 25, 129
Beechdrops, 119
Berries, 26, 27
Biennial plant, 22
Biodegradable, 34
Birch, 119, 131
Bittersweet, 26, 27
Black swallowtail butterfly, 81
Black-eyed susan, 81
Blackberry, 2, 26, 27
Blackfly larva, 37
Bladderwort, 37, 39–40
Box turtle, 119
Breathing, underwater, 59–60
Brown snake, 2
Bullhead, 46
Burdock, 2
Bush honeysuckle, 27
Butterfly,
   chrysalid, 105
   ecological significance of, 105

Cactus wren nest, 175
Cactus, 159, 174
Caddisfly larva, 46, 56, 65
Camouflage, 67–68
Cardinal territories, 107
Caterpillars, 119, 177
   care of, 106, 141
   relationship with trees, 139–42

Cattail, 37
Centipede, 2, 14, 103
CFCs, 155
Chickadee, 119, 143
Chipmunk, 21, 24
Chlorofluorocarbons, 155
Chlorophyll, 87, 136. *See also* Photosynthesis
Chokecherry, 26, 81
Chrysalid, 105
Cicada, 2, 5–6
Clear-cutting, 153
Colonizing, of plants, 96
Color change in leaves, 135
Compaction, of soil, 17
Composting, 31–32,
Copepod, 73
Coyote, 81,108, 159, 178
Crab grass, 2
Crabapple, 2, 26
Crayfish, 37
Creosote bush, 159
Cricket, 14

Dace, 37, 39
Daddy-longlegs, 81
Daisy fleabane, 81
Dams, effects on fish, 49–50
Damselfly, 37, 63
Damselfly nymph, 60, 69
Dandelion, 2, 24
Dandelion seed, 95
Daphnia, 73
Deadly nightshade, 26, 27
Deer mouse, 119, 144
Deer, 119
Diversity, 129
   of plants, 100
Diving beetle, 46, 62
Dragonfly, 37, 62–63
Dragonfly nymph, 60, 62, 68–69
Drip irrigation, 184
Duckweed, 37

Earthworm, 2, 14, 15, 20–21
Ectotherms, 176
Elderberry, 25
Electric meter, 111–12
Elodea, 70, 71
Endangered ecosystems, 178, 179
Endangered species, 179
Energy
   measuring amounts of, 111
   cutting back, 113–14
English sparrow, 2

Erosion, 18-20, 152
Evening primrose, 159
Evolution, 163, 178
    of cactus, 175

Fairy shrimp, 53
Ferns, 119
Field juniper, 2–4
Fish, 52, 60
    coloration of, 68
Flashlight, 75
Flow chart, 27
Flower, 85
Flowers
    nectar guides of, 93
    parts of, 91
    pollination of, 89
    of trees, 130
Fluorescent light bulbs, 114
Flying squirrel, 119, 144, 14
Food chains, 108
    meat-eating, 109
    in pond, 70, 73
    sunlight as initial source, 85
Fox squirrel, 2
Forcing tree buds, 130
Freshwater mussel, 37, 39
Frog, 37, 52, 55, 65, 74
Fungi, 120, 152, 162. See also Mushrooms

Gall insects, 119, 138
Galls, 154
Gardening, ecological, 115
Garter snake, 2
Giant water bug, 62
Goldenrod, 81, 92
Gopher tortoise, 159
Grackle, 37, 65
Grapevines, 145
Grass clippings, 32
Grasses, 81
Grey squirrel, 2
Ground beetle, 14, 103
Growth rings
    on branches, 123
    on trunk wood, 123, 124
Gypsy moths, 140

Habitats, 105, 136
Harvestman, 81
Hemlock, 119
Heron, 37, 52, 64
Hickory, 25
Homes, 11-12, 45, 144, 146 , 174. See also Habitats
    in streams, 45
Honeybee, 84, 90
    behavior of, 89, 92–93, 94
Hornbeam, 119

Huckleberry, 119
Hummingbird, 93, 179
Hunting spider, 56
Hydra, 73
Hyphae 146. See also Fungi

Indian pipe, 119, 120–21
Indicators, plants as, 23
Introduced animals, 6

Jackrabbits, 177
Japanese beetle, 2, 6–7, 142
Jays, as seed dispersers, 133
Journal-keeping, 8
Juice boxes, 34
Juniper, 26, 81
Junk mail, 34

Katydid, 119
Kingfisher, 52

Lacewing larva, 101
Lady bug, 81, 101
Lamb's-quarters, 2
Landfill, 51
Leaves
    adaptations of, 10, 71, 88, 170
        to light, 88–89
    breakdown of, 28–29
    color change of, 135
    conserving moisture, 170
    transpiration, 126
Lichens, 136, 137,159, 162
Litter, 28, 29,
Little bluestem grass, 2
Liverwort, 37
Lupine, 159, 160–61

Making models
    of camouflaged pond animals, 67–68
    of soil erosion, 48,
    of streambed, 41–42
Maple, 25 119
Maple seed, 95
Maple gall, 138
Maps, 75, 104
Marking, to observe behavior, 67
Mayfly, 37
Mayfly nymph, 60, 61
Meadow mouse, 2, 81, 103, 104
Merlin, 118
Microscope, 72
Migration, of ocean fish, 49
Milkweed, 81, 82
Milkweed beetle, 81, 82
Milkweed seed, 95
Millipede, 2, 103
Mink, 52, 64, 65
Mockingbird, 159

Mole, 2, 20–21, 24
Monarch butterfly, 81, 82, 177
Mosquito, 37, 58
Mosquito larva, 69
Moss, 37
Mourning dove, 159
Mullein, 88, 159
Mushroom, 119, 146, 147. *See also* Mycellium,
    Mycorrhizae, and Hyphae
Muskrat, 64
Mussel, 64, 65
Mustards, 24–25
Mycellium, 15, 121. *See also* Hyphae
Mycorrhizae, 147

Nectar guides, 93
Niches, 100
Northern bush-honeysuckle, 2
Norway maple, 2
Nutrients, 36, 45, 49, 51, 127, 128, 148, 149, 173,
    180
    excess of, 48–49
    flowing from roots, 87
    in pond water, 39
    recycled by trees, 118
    in the soil, 19, 21

Oak, 25, 119, 129, 140, 159
Oak galls, 138
Oak seeds, 133
Oak twig pruner beetle, 122
Old-growth forests, 153
Ovenbird, 119
Owl nests, finding, 108
Ox-eye daisy, 81

Painted turtle, 37
Paper bags, decompostion, 34
pH, 149, 150–51
Pheromone, 7
Phloem cells, 124
Photosynthesis, 86. *See also* Food chains
Pigeon, 2
Pillbug, 14
Pin oak, 2
Pitch pine, 159
Pine, 25, 119, 131–32, 133, 166
Planaria, 73
Plankton, 39, 53, 72, 73
Plantain, 2, 18, 24
Plastic, problems with, 29, 32–33
Plastic bags, 34
Podomogetan, 37, 71
Pokeberry, 27
Pollination, 89
    description of, 90–91
Pollution, 30, 53, 155, 180, 185
    acid precipitation, 76

Poplar, 25, 81, 129
Precycling, 34
Predators, 73, 108, 118, 139, 177–78
    aquatic, 61
    defense from, 172, 176–77
    problems of spear-fishing, 63
    signs of at the water's edge, 65–66
Protein combinations in food, 115
Protractor, 168
Purification of water systems, 50–51
Purple cabbage indicator, 150

Queen Anne's lace, 2, 22–23, 92

Rabbit
    cottontail, 81,177
    jackrabbit, 177
Raccoon, 2, 37, 64
Ragweed, 2
Raspberry, 2
Recycling, 30, 31, 32
    of paper products, 153
Red cedar, 2
Red eft, 37, 119
Red fox, 81
Red maple, 37
Red-cabbage water, 77
Red-spotted newt, 37
Respiration
    in photosynthesis, 87
    in water plants, 70
Rhododendron, 166
Road salt, 155
Robin, 27, 143
Robin territories, 107
Root hairs, 125
Roots
    growth of, 125
    water movement through, 126
Rose, 25, 26, 81
Rosette, 22, 23, 88, 171
Rotifer, 73
Rotting, 28, 30–31,32, 149
    of wood, 127–28
Runoff, agricultural, 49

Sagebrush, 159
Salamander, 15 , 37
Salamander larva, 60
Sassafras, 129
Scrub oak, 159
Sediment distributions, 44
Seedbanks, 179
Seeds
    flying, 95-96
    hitchhiking, 96
    nuts as, 133, 134, 135
Shiner, 46

Shrew, 20–21, 119
Skunk cabbage, 37
Skunk, 2
Slug, 15
Snail, 14, 37, 66, 69
Snapping turtle, 62
Succotash, 116
Soil
    acidity of, 150
    compacted, 17
    and decomposition, 28, 149
    as filter, 183
    sandy, 164
    heat-retention of, 168
    moisture-retention of, 165
    water-retention of, 181–82
Soil-testing kit, 77
Song sparrow, 81
Sowbug, 2, 14, 103
Sparrow hawk, 81, 108
Spider eggs, 14
Spider wasp, 159
Spider, 75, 81
    funnel-weaving, 15
    orb-weaver, 83–84
    trapdoor, 159
    wolf, 15
Spiderwebs, 84
Spotted salamander, 74
Spotted sandpiper, 65
Starling, 2, 6–7
Stonefly, 37
Streambed, 41, 43–45
Streamlining, 46–47
Stress, environmental, 154
Succession, 24–25, 26, 145
    in a field, 98
    in a pond, 53
Sugar, 136, 179
    in plants, 87
Sumac, 25, 81, 97
Sunfish, 37, 68
Surface tension, of water, 56, 57, 58
Survey, 9, 24
    of diversity, 101
    of pond life, 52, 54
    of town lands, 104
    of woodland birds, 143
Swamp loosestrife, 37
Sweet fern, 159
Swimming adaptations, 68–69
Sycamore, seed, 95

Tadploe, 60
Tanager, 119

Temperature, 166
    regulation of, 176
Tent caterpillar, 81
Territorial behavior
    of birds, 106–107
    of insects, 107
    of mammals, 107–108
Thermometer, 44, 167–68
Thrush, 119
Tiger beetle, 159
Toad, 37
Topsoil, 18, 47–48, 163
    loss of, 19, 47–48
Toxic wastes, 182, 185
Toxins, 82, 97 172, 174
    in plants, 82, 139
Tracks, of animals, 11
Transpiration, 126
Trees, double-trunk, 145
Tropical hardwoods, 153
Tropical rain forests, 153
    products from, 180
Truffles, 148
Tumbleweed, 159
Tundra, 159
Turtle, 52, 55–56, 59

Variation, in plants, 92
Vines, 26
Violet, 119
Vireo, 119
Vole, 2, 81, 103, 104
Vulture 159

Water beetle, 46
Water boatman, 69
Water scorpion, 60
Water snake, 37, 52, 65
Water strider, 37, 54–55, 57, 58
Water table, 182
Water tiger, 69
Water lily, 56, 71
Watershed, 75
Whirligig beetle, 37, 55, 57, 58
Willow, 37
Witch hazel gall, 138
Woodchuck, 24, 81
Woodfrog, 119
Woodpecker, 119, 143, 174
Woolly bear caterpillar, 2
Writing paper, problems with, 32, 33

Xylem, 124, 126

Yellow jacket, 2, 4–5, 13
Yew, 2
Yucca, 159

About the Author

Jorie Hunken has been teaching children and adults about nature and the environment for more than thirty years. For twenty-five of those years, she worked in the Boston area, teaching at various museums, schools, camps, and conferences and working with such organizations as the New England Wild Flower Society, the Boston Children's Museum, Fayerweather Street School, and the Appalachian Mountain Club. She currently enjoys her family, her community, and the plants and animals of Woodstock, Connecticut.